Reading for the Gifted Student

Challenging Activities for the Advanced Learner

Written by **Danielle Denega**

Illustrations by **Jackie Snider**

An imprint of Sterling Children's Books

Whether your student has been identified as gifted and talented or is simply a scholastic overachiever, school-assigned activities may not be challenging enough for him or her. To keep your student engaged in learning, it is important to provide reading activities that quench his or her thirst for information and allow opportunities to exercise critical thinking.

This workbook contains much more than typical reading passages and questions; it does not rely on the assumption that a gifted and talented sixth-grader simply requires seventh-grade work. Instead, the nearly 200 pages of reading passages, comprehension questions, and creative activities are calibrated to match the average reading level, analytical capacity, and subject interest of this specialized group of learners. Specifically, the vocabulary, sentence structure, and length of passages in this grade 6 workbook are set at levels normally appropriate for grades 7 and 8, but the comprehension skills increase in difficulty as the workbook progresses, starting with grade 6 curriculum standards and working through those associated with grade 7. The passages' topics are primarily nonfiction and present concepts, themes, and issues fundamental to all disciplines, including science, social studies, health, and the arts.

Question formats range from multiple choice and short answer to true-or-false, fill-in-the-blank, and much more. Also sprinkled throughout the workbook are creative activities that will encourage your student to write a story or draw a picture. Your student may check his or her work against the answer key near the end of the workbook, but you may wish to review it together, since many questions have numerous possible answers.

Reading, writing, and language skills are essential to any student's academic success. By utilizing this workbook, you are providing your gifted learner an opportunity to seek new challenges and experience learning at an advanced level.

Contents

Purebred Administration

The neighborhood dogs were preparing for the annual election to decide who would be the next president of the Canine Association. Pugsly told his friend Higgins, "You know, you should run this year. Poodle is running for the Purebred Party, but I think it's time we had a Mutt in office. I mean, what have the Purebreds really done to make life better for us?"

Higgins looked at Pugsly skeptically and replied, "Really? You think the Mutts have a shot this year? I do have many ideas that I think would truly improve our standard of living. But what purebred dog would elect me? There's never been a Mutt Administration around here. And I fear that others won't be open to a new way of doing things."

"Well, I'm a purebred Pug and I would vote for you!" Pugsly encouraged Higgins. "I think this neighborhood is tired of being fed the same old food—I know I am." Higgins nodded at Pugsly. "You're right! That Poodle is all bark and no bite. She's promising things like unlimited treats, a no-leash law, and even tempting all the dogs by telling them she would ban flea medication. There's just no way she could realistically make those things happen, and, anyway, those things wouldn't necessarily be good for us."

Pugsly wagged his tail. "That settles it, Higgins. You are running for president!" Pugsly began running from yard to yard to inform the other members of the Canine Association that Poodle was going to have some competition. But the reactions to this news were mixed.

The Wheaton Terrier scoffed, "Imagine that. A mutt in office! Everyone knows you can't trust a mutt!" and the Beagle turned up his nose and responded, "I will never vote for a common mutt. I want a dog like me—a purebred—to represent my best interests. A mutt simply would not understand my beliefs!"

The Yorkipoo questioned, "What's Higgins's platform? I need to understand what he'll do for the greater good before I can back him instead of Poodle. I can't simply agree to vote for him just because I, too, am a mutt." But the Shepherd-Labrador mix enthusiastically told Pugsly, "It's about time there was a mutt in office! I don't care who he is or what he thinks, we have just got to get those Purebreds out of there!"

Finally, Pugsly approached Poodle, who was napping on the window-seat of the mansion in which she lived. Pugsly pawed the glass to wake her and explained, "Higgins from down the block is going to run for president of the Canine Association, too. Many of the dogs in the neighborhood are open to the idea."

Poodle yawned and stretched her long legs, licked a stray hair back into its proper place, and then coolly said, "Waddle off, Pugsly. You and I both know that I'm a paw-in to win the election. We have had a poodle in office for the past two terms, and before that, an endless string of other purebreds. Besides, what dog in his right mind wouldn't want a no-leash law? So tell that Higgins to put his tail between his legs and go back to his doghouse." Pugsly snorted, spraying the windowpane, turned tail, and walked away, "We'll see about that, Poodle. I'd be on your pads if I were you."

Answer the questions about the story.

1. How would you describe Poodle?

_____

2. How would you describe Higgins?

_____

3. How would you describe Pugsly?

_____

4. How did the Wheaton Terrier respond to Pugsly's news?

_____

_____

5. How did the Yorkipoo respond?

_____

_____

6. How did the Shepherd-Labrador mix respond to the news?

_____

7. Do you think that any of these responses is right or wrong? Explain.

_____

_____

8. What do you think of Poodle's campaign promises?

_____

9. How does Poodle react to Pugsly's news?

_____

10. Do you think this situation applies to the human world? Explain.

_____

_____

_____

Canine Campaign

Now that Poodle and Higgins are competing for the presidency of the Canine Association, the election campaign has become tense. Both candidates' supporters have posted fliers around town in an effort to sway voters' opinions.

1

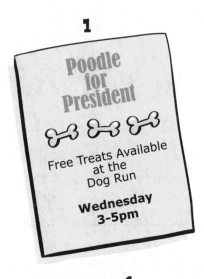

Poodle for President

Free Treats Available at the Dog Run

Wednesday 3-5pm

2

Higgins for President

There's a New Dog in Town
Vote for the Canine who will effect change!

3

Vote for Higgins !

Higgins will:

✓ Improve the water quality at the dog run

✓ Lengthen the no-leash weekend hours at Rococo Beach

4

Higgins Voice of the Common Dog

He will support ALL dogs, not just the privileged!

5

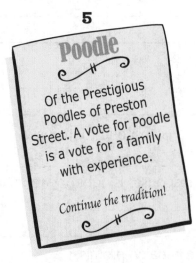

Poodle

Of the Prestigious Poodles of Preston Street. A vote for Poodle is a vote for a family with experience.

Continue the tradition!

6

Vote Poodle

Simply the Best Should Lead

7

Poodle Administration

Never wear a leash again - anytime or anywhere!

Answer the questions about the fliers.

1. What tactic does flier 1 use? Do you think it will draw voters?

_____

2. Do you think that flier 7 promises something realistic? Explain.

_____

_____

3. What tone does flier 6 express? _____

superiority   inferiority   mediocrity

4. How would you describe the tone of flier 4? Write the letter of the answer on the line. _____

a. lowly   **b.** submissive   **c.** righteous

5. What do you think flier 2 means? Explain.

_____

_____

6. Compare flier 3 to flier 7. Which do you find more appealing?

_____

7. Do you find flier 5 persuasive? Why or why not?

_____

_____

8. What is the overall goal of posting such fliers before an election?

_____

9. Whom would you vote for in the Canine Association election?

_____

10. Can you think of any American families that have been leaders, the way the Poodle family has?

_____

Presidential Poster

Imagine that you are running for president of the student body. What aspects of student life would you change? What would you keep the same? Why are you better than the other candidates? Use the space below to create your own campaign flier. Be specific so that readers will know what you stand for.

Candidate Cons (and Pros!)

1. Research the most recent U.S. presidential election using various sources, such as newspapers, magazines, the Internet, and books. Read as much as you can about the two most prominent candidates. Write the pros and cons for each one in the chart.

Candidate 1: _____	Candidate 2: _____
Pro	
Con	
Pro	
Con	
Pro	
Con	
Pro	
Con	

2. Analyze the chart. Did the candidates share the same number of pros and cons? Or did one of the candidates have more pros or cons?

_____

3. If the second option is true, what does that tell you about that candidate?

_____

4. Imagine that you were old enough to vote. Your vote is significant, so it is important to make the right choice between the candidates. Who would you choose and why?

_____

5. Was there a different, less prominent candidate in the election? Who was it?

_____

6. Why do you think that candidate was given less attention?

_____

_____

7. What does that tell you about the American political system? Do you think this is good or bad? Explain.

_____

_____

The Makings of Mascots

There are two animals more famous in politics than any others: the Democratic donkey and the Republican elephant. These animals have been the symbols of America's two main political parties since the 1800s. But how did they come to represent American politics?

The Democratic donkey was first associated with Democrat Andrew Jackson's 1828 presidential campaign. His opponents likened him to a donkey because of his populist views and slogan, "Let the people rule." So Jackson decided to use the image of the strong-willed animal on his campaign posters. Because of his reputation for stubbornness, the image stuck with him during his presidency.

Three decades later, the animal appeared in an 1870 *Harper's Weekly* cartoon drawn by cartoonist Thomas Nast. The symbol caught the public imagination and he continued to use it to represent pro-Democrat editors and newspapers. By the 1880 presidential campaign, the donkey had become firmly established as a political symbol of the Democratic Party.

Thomas Nast is also credited with helping the elephant become the symbol of the Republican Party. In 1874, Nast published a cartoon in *Harper's Weekly* that featured a donkey clothed in lion's skin, scaring away other animals. One of those animals was an elephant that bore the label "The Republican Vote."

After that year's mid-term elections, in which the Republicans did particularly badly, Nast drew another elephant to illustrate how the Republican vote had been enticed away from its normal allegiance. After that, the elephant became associated with the Republican Party.

Answer the questions about the reading.

1. What is the Republican Party's animal mascot?

_____

2. When you picture that animal in your head, what traits come to mind?

_____

3. What is the Democratic Party's animal mascot?

_____

4. When you picture that animal in your head, what traits come to mind?

_____

5. Who is the cartoonist credited with popularizing these symbols?

_____

6. In what publication did these pictures appear?

_____

7. In what years did the cartoons first appear?

_____

8. Which president was called a donkey?

_____

9. If you could choose animals to represent these parties today, which animals would you pick for each and why?

_____

_____

10. If you had to choose an animal to represent yourself, which animal would it be and why?

_____

_____

Why Tuesday?

In 1845, Election Day in the United States was deemed the first Tuesday after the first Monday in November. However, many people today feel that a random Tuesday in the autumn doesn't suit modern voters' needs. While voters can entertain the possibility of changing Election Day to a weekend day, weekend voting wouldn't be suitable, either.

That Tuesday in November was chosen for several reasons. In the beginning of America's history, people survived by farming, and so lawmakers considered the agrarian lifestyle to determine that November was the most convenient month for farmers and rural workers to travel to the polls. At that point in the year, the fall harvest was over—a time-consuming task for most voters. And in most parts of the country, the weather was still mild enough to permit voters to travel without fear of inclement weather.

A second travel consideration was distance: Most residents of rural America needed to travel a long way to the county seat. Monday was not an option, because many people would have to begin traveling on Sunday, and this would have conflicted with Church services and Sunday worship. Thus Tuesday was the first convenient day of the week.

But other important days in the month of November had to be considered as well. Election Day couldn't fall on the first of November for two reasons: November 1 is All Saint's Day, which is a holy day for Christians, and also the day of the month that merchants traditionally reserved for balancing their books and taking inventory.

But this tradition invites rethinking: why Tuesday? As Americans have become urbanized and motorized, more polling places have been established close to voters' homes. It is less important to hold elections on Tuesdays. However, average voter turnout is very low, contrasted with other democracies. Would a weekend day possibly be better as Election Day? Most other democracies hold elections on weekends.

The answer is no! There is simply too much else for voters to do on weekends. For working Americans, weekends are a designated time for family obligations and errands, as well as recreational activities. Voters are just as unlikely to find time on a Saturday or Sunday to vote as they would on a Tuesday. Workdays are actually better for voting, because those days tend to be more organized. People in the United States often adhere to a more specific schedule during the week because of work and school hours. Therefore, shifting our elections to weekends would have little effect on voter turnout.

Answer the questions about the reading.

1. What is the opinion expressed in this reading?

_____

_____

2. Do you think that the author supports his or her opinion with enough reasons? Explain.

_____

_____

3. Do you agree or disagree with the author on this issue? _____

4. What reasons do you think the author had for writing this passage? Circle all that apply.

    to inform   to persuade   to entertain   to offend

5. What does the word *inclement* in paragraph 2 mean?

_____

6. Circle the words below that can be used to express a strong opinion.

          never   always   sometimes

7. When was Election Day chosen? _____

8. What were two reasons why that day was chosen?

_____

_____

9. What is one reason why the author claims that a Saturday or Sunday would **not** be a better day?

_____

_____

10. If you could assign a new day for Election Day, what day would you choose and why?

_____

_____

_____

15

Plant Cells

Amyloplast: organelle that stores starch; found in starchy plants like tubers and fruits.

Cell membrane: thin layer of protein and fat that surrounds the cell, but is inside the cell wall; semipermeable, allowing some substances to pass into the cell and blocking others.

Cell wall: thick, rigid membrane that surrounds a plant cell and gives the cell most of its support and structure; bonds with other cell walls to form the structure of the plant.

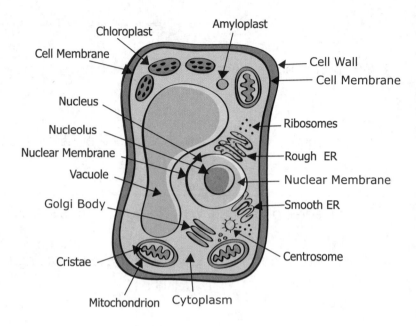

Centrosome: small body located near the nucleus; has dense center and radiating tubules; during cell division, or mitosis, it divides into two parts that move to opposite sides of the dividing cell.

Chloroplast: elongated or disc-shaped organelle containing chlorophyll; where photosynthesis occurs.

Cristae: folded inner membrane of a plant cell's mitochondrion; its walls are the site of the cell's energy production—where ATP is generated.

Cytoplasm: jelly-like material outside the cell nucleus in which the organelles are located.

Golgi body: flattened, layered, sac-like organelle; resembles a stack of pancakes and located near the nucleus; packages proteins and carbohydrates into membrane-bound vesicles for export from the cell.

Mitochondrion: spherical or rod-shaped organelle with a double membrane; its inner membrane is infolded many times, forming a series of projections called cristae; by respiration, converts the energy stored in glucose into ATP, or adenosine triphosphate, for the cell to use as energy.

Nucleus: spherical body containing many organelles, including the nucleolus; surrounded by the nuclear membrane; by controlling protein synthesis, it controls many of the functions of the cell; contains DNA, in chromosomes.

Nuclear membrane: membrane that surrounds the nucleus.

Nucleolus: organelle within the nucleus; where ribosomal RNA is produced.

Ribosome: small organelle composed of cytoplasmic granules; sites of protein synthesis.

Rough endoplasmic reticulum (rough ER): vast system of interconnected, membranous, infolded, and convoluted sacs; located in the cell's cytoplasm; covered with ribosomes, giving it a rough appearance; transports materials through the cell and produces proteins.

Smooth endoplasmic reticulum (smooth ER): vast system of interconnected, membranous, infolded, and convoluted tubes; located in the cytoplasm; transports materials through the cell; contains enzymes and produces and digests lipids, or fats, and membrane proteins; buds off from rough ER, moving the newly-made proteins and lipids to the Golgi body and membranes.

Vacuole: large, membrane-bound space; filled with fluid; a single vacuole often takes up much of the cell; helps maintain the shape of the cell.

Answer the questions about plant cells.

1. What is the term for the process by which energy from sunlight is converted into chemical energy, or food? _____ In what part of the cell does this occur? _____

2. What might happen to the cell without these? _____
   _____

3. What two parts of the plant cell help maintain its shape and structure?
   _____

4. What is the process of cell division called? _____

5. What part of the cell acts as a goalie, allowing some things in and blocking others?
   _____

6. What is one difference between smooth ER and rough ER?
   _____
   _____

7. Which of the following are **not** found in plant cells? _____
   mitochondrion   ribosome   lysosome

Animal Cells

Cell membrane: thin layer of protein and fat that surrounds the cell; semipermeable, allowing some substances to pass into the cell and blocking others.

Centrosome: small body located near the nucleus; has a dense center and radiating tubules; site of microtubule production; during cell division, or mitosis, it divides into two parts that move to opposite sides of the dividing cell.

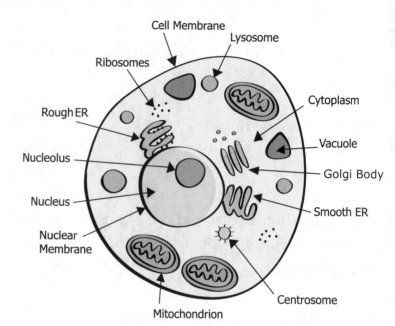

Cytoplasm: jelly-like material outside the cell nucleus in which the organelles are located.

Golgi body: flattened, layered, sac-like organelle; resembles a stack of pancakes; located near the nucleus; produces the membranes that surround the lysosomes and packages proteins and carbohydrates into membrane-bound vesicles for export from the cell.

Lysosome: round organelle surrounded by a membrane; contains digestive enzymes; site of digestion of cell nutrients.

Mitochondrion: spherical or rod-shaped organelle with a double membrane; inner membrane is infolded many times, forming a series of projections called cristae; converts the energy stored in glucose into ATP, or adenosine triphosphate, for the cell to use as energy.

Nuclear membrane: membrane that surrounds the nucleus.

Nucleolus: organelle within the nucleus; may be more than one present; where ribosomal RNA is produced.

Nucleus: spherical body containing many organelles, including the nucleolus; surrounded by the nuclear membrane; by controlling protein synthesis, controls many of the functions of the cell; contains DNA, in chromosomes.

Ribosome: small organelle composed of cytoplasmic granules; site of protein synthesis.

Rough endoplasmic reticulum (rough ER): vast system of interconnected and convoluted sacs located in the cell's cytoplasm; covered with ribosomes; transports materials through the cell and produces proteins in sacs called cisternae.

Smooth endoplasmic reticulum (smooth ER): vast system of interconnected, convoluted tubes located in the cytoplasm; transports materials through the cell; contains enzymes and produces and digests lipids, or fats, and membrane proteins; smooth ER buds off from rough ER, moving the newly-made proteins and lipids to the Golgi body, lysosomes, and membranes.

Vacuole: fluid-filled, membrane-surrounded cavity inside a cell; filled with digesting food and waste material on its way out of the cell.

Use the descriptions and diagram to compare and contrast the animal cell to the plant cell on page 16. If a statement below applies to a plant cell, mark it with a *P*. If it applies to an animal cell, mark it with an *A*. Mark it with a *B* if it applies to both plant and animal cells.

1. I contain lysosomes. _____

2. I perform photosynthesis. _____

3. I often have one large vacuole. _____

4. My organelles are found in cytoplasm. _____

5. I have no cell wall. _____

6. My nucleus controls many of my functions. _____

Answer the questions about animal cells.

7. Which organelle in an animal cell is somewhat like a stomach? _____

8. Which part of the cell is sort of like its brain? _____

9. What organelle is the trash can of the cell? _____

10. What organelles are the energy powerhouses of the cell? _____

Bacteria

Bacteria are microscopic, unicellular organisms. Bacteria are part of the Kingdom *Monera*, which is a word meaning "solitary" or "alone." Bacteria are also primitive organisms. In fact, they were among the very first living things to appear on earth. A scientist named Antony van Leeuwenhoek made the world aware of the existence of bacteria when he observed them under a microscope in the 1600s.

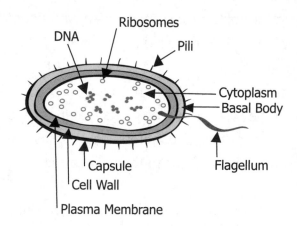

Bacteria are prokaryotic organisms, which makes the bacteria cell quite different from plant and animal cells. Bacteria lack a nucleus and other membrane-bound organelles, except ribosomes. Unlike animals and plants, bacteria have pili and flagella—or hairs and tails—and most have a cell capsule.

There are many different types of bacteria: rod-shaped, round, and spiral-shaped. Some bacteria—called aerobic bacteria—need atmospheric oxygen to live, but others do not. These are called anaerobic bacteria, and they acquire their oxygen from other molecular compounds.

Bacteria are found almost everywhere on earth, including in the seas and lakes. In fact, bacteria even live in ocean canyons and trenches that are more than 32,800 feet deep. Bacteria live in the soil, in the tissue of plants and animals, and on every continent on earth, including frigid Antarctica.

Bacteria generally have a bad reputation. They travel very fast and cause illnesses, such as strep throat, and harmful red tide seen in lakes. However, bacteria also serve many positive purposes, including releasing nitrogen to plants and decomposing organic material. Bacteria help the fermentation process used in the production of cheese and yogurt.

Bacteria grow rapidly and are resilient organisms. They grow in colonies and reproduce by asexual budding or fission, in which the cell increases in size and then splits in two. Bacteria can survive conditions that would kill most other organisms. This is because they take a nap. Well, not exactly, but in the right conditions, bacteria develop a thick outer wall and enter a dormant phase, thereby protecting themselves from harm. That's why people have to use disinfectants with strong chemicals to kill bacteria as they clean.

As for diet, some bacteria are heterotrophs, which means that they eat other organisms. Most heterotrophic bacteria are saprobes, which means they absorb dead organic material like rotting flesh. Other bacteria are autotrophs, which means they make their own food. They do this either through photosynthesis or chemosynthesis, a process that uses carbon dioxide, water, and chemicals to make food.

Answer the questions about the reading.

1. What does the word *microscopic* in paragraph 1 mean?

_____

2. What does the word *unicellular* in paragraph 1 mean?

_____

3. Why do you think bacteria were given the name *Monera*?

_____

4. What is the singular form of *bacteria*?

_____

5. What is the difference between *aerobic* and *anaerobic*?

_____

_____

6. List three differences between bacteria cells and plant or animal cells.

_____

_____

_____

7. Are bacteria in your house? Explain.

_____

_____

8. Underline the words below that describe bacteria.

swift	fragile	hardy	robust	pokey
useful	sluggish	hazardous	delicate	

9. Why do we need to clean with strong disinfectants?

_____

_____

10. What might bacteria like to find for lunch?

_____

A Great American

Thomas Jefferson was a true Renaissance man and a fresh voice for America. Jefferson was not simply the third president of the United States; he was also a historian, philosopher, lawyer, scientist, author, architect, inventor, and statesman. Jefferson could speak five languages fluently and was able to read in two additional ones. He was the author of the Declaration of Independence and the Statute of Virginia for Religious Freedom, as well as the founder of the University of Virginia. In these ways, Jefferson served and enriched his country for more than five decades.

Jefferson was born in Albemarle County, Virginia, on April 13, 1743. His father was a successful planter and surveyor and his mother hailed from one of Virginia's most distinguished families. He attended William and Mary College in Williamsburg at sixteen years old, and afterward studied law.

In his early professional life, Jefferson practiced law and served in local government as a magistrate, county lieutenant, and member of the House of Burgesses. Jefferson was also a member of the Continental Congress and chosen in 1776 to draft the Declaration of Independence.

In June 1779 he succeeded Patrick Henry as governor of Virginia. By 1781, Jefferson had moved into his now-famous home at Monticello. Jefferson had inherited land from his father, and began building Monticello when he was just twenty-six. He lived there with his wife, Martha, until her death in 1782. The couple had six children together, and Jefferson greatly mourned the loss of his wife. He never remarried, and he stayed in Monticello for the rest of his life.

In 1789, Thomas Jefferson accepted the post of secretary of state under George Washington. Then, in 1796, he became vice president after losing the presidential election to John Adams by three electoral votes. But just four years later, he defeated Adams and became president of the United States. As president, Jefferson purchased the Louisiana Territory and supported the Lewis and Clark Expedition.

In 1809, Jefferson was succeeded by James Madison. After his presidency, Jefferson continued to serve his country in various ways. He sold his collection of books to the government to form the core of the Library of Congress. He also founded the University of Virginia, a project that included spearheading the legislative campaign for its charter, securing its location, designing its buildings, and planning its curriculum.

Jefferson died on July 4, 1826, at the age of eighty-three. It was the fiftieth anniversary of the signing of the Declaration of Independence. Just hours later, his close friend John Adams also passed away.

Answer the questions about the reading.

1. Place a check next to the phrase that best describes the author's purpose for this reading.

_____ to persuade _____ to entertain _____ to inform

2. Number the events in the correct order.

_____ Jefferson died on July 4, 1826, at the age of eighty-three.

_____ Jefferson was also a member of the Continental Congress and chosen in 1776 to draft the Declaration of Independence.

_____ Jefferson was born in Albemarle County, Virginia, on April 13, 1743.

_____ As president, Jefferson purchased the Louisiana Territory and supported the Lewis and Clark Expedition.

_____ He sold his collection of books to the government to form the core of the Library of Congress.

3. What do you think the phrase *Renaissance man* in paragraph 1 means?

_____

4. Underline the name of the university that Jefferson founded.

5. Circle the roles below for which Thomas Jefferson was qualified.

painter   architect   president   dentist

inventor   lawyer   sculptor

6. What does the word *enriched* in paragraph 1 mean?

_____

7. What three events made July 4, 1826, significant?

_____

_____

_____

8. Name three other great Americans mentioned in the reading.

_____

9. What was the name of Thomas Jefferson's home? _____

10. Name two important things Jefferson accomplished during his time as president of the United States.

_____

_____

Lewis and Clark's Trail

The Lewis and Clark Expedition was the first United States overland exploration of the Pacific Northwest Coast. Its two leaders were Meriwether Lewis and William Clark. In all, the Lewis and Clark Expedition covered about 8,000 miles, starting and ending in St. Louis, Missouri. Its main goal was to locate a route that would allow for America to expand westward.

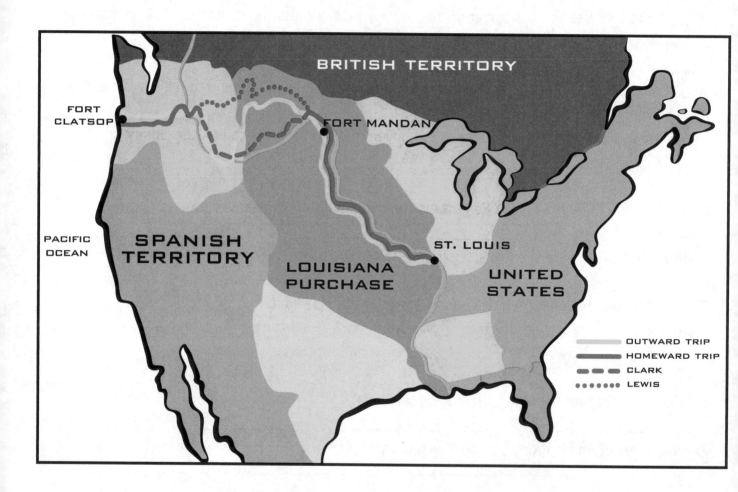

Answer the questions about the reading and the map.

1. Circle the word below that describes Lewis and Clark's expedition.

exploratory   common   quick

2. What was the main purpose of the Lewis and Clark Expedition?

_____

_____

3. In what state did the expedition begin? _____

4. What large body of water did the explorers reach before returning home? _____

5. Lewis and Clark explored Spanish Territory during their expedition. *True* or *false*?

_____

6. Up which river did the expedition travel for quite a while? _____

7. How many miles did the Lewis and Clark Expedition cover? _____

8. What purpose would this map serve a reader? Write the letter of the answer on the line. ____
   a. to laugh heartily
   b. to acquire information about the expedition
   c. to persuade others to follow the same route

9. Place a check next to the word(s) that is a synonym for *expedition*.
   ____ ship   ____ journey   ____ wagon   ____ voyage   ____ trip

10. Lewis and Clark were brave to embark on this expedition. *Fact* or *opinion*?

_____

Trail Timeline

The following is a timeline of some of the highlights of Lewis and Clark's expedition.

January 18, 1803
U.S. President Thomas Jefferson sends a secret message to Congress in which he asks for approval and funding of an expedition, called the Corps of Discovery, to explore the western part of North America.

May 14, 1804
The Corps of Discovery, as the Lewis and Clark Expedition was known, begins its journey up the Missouri River.

July 4, 1804
The Corps holds the first Independence Day celebration west of the Mississippi River.

August 3, 1804
The Corps holds a council with the Oto and Missouri tribes.

August 20, 1804
Sergeant Charles Floyd dies of natural causes; he is the only fatality among the Corps of Discovery during the expedition.

September 1804
The Corps enters the Great Plains and sees animals unknown in the eastern United States.

November 4, 1804
Lewis and Clark hire French-Canadian fur-trader Toussaint Charbonneau and his Shoshone wife, Sacagawea, to act as guides and interpreters.

December 24, 1804
The explorers finish building Fort Mandan, their winter quarters in present-day North Dakota.

February 11, 1805
Sacagawea's son, Jean Baptiste Charbonneau, is born.

May 16, 1805
One of their boats nearly overturns, and Lewis credits Sacagawea with saving their most important possessions.

May 31, 1805
The Corps reaches the White Cliffs region of the Missouri River.

June 13, 1805
Lewis reaches the Great Falls of the Missouri.

July 1805
The expedition reaches the Three Forks of the Missouri, which they name the Jefferson, Gallatin, and Madison in honor of the current U.S. president, secretary of the treasury, and secretary of state.

August 12, 1805
Lewis finds the headwaters of the Missouri River. He then crosses the Continental Divide and Lemhi Pass and discovers that there is no Northwest Passage.

August 17, 1805
The main party arrives at the Shoshone camp, where Sacagawea recognizes the chief as her brother.

September 11, 1805
The Corps begins the steep ascent into the Bitterroot Range of the Rocky Mountains; the crossing will cover more than 160 miles.

September 23, 1805
Starving, the travelers emerge from the mountains near present-day Weippe, Idaho, at the villages of the Nez Perce.

October 16, 1805
The expedition reaches the Columbia River, the last waterway to the Pacific Ocean.

November 24, 1805
Having reached the Pacific, the expedition builds their winter quarters. The encampment was later called Fort Clatsop.

March 23, 1806
The team sets out for home.

Answer the questions about the reading and the map.

1. Match each date to the event that occurred.

May 14, 1804	Lewis and Clark hire Toussaint Charbonneau and Sacagawea to act as guides and interpreters.
November 4, 1804	The Corps of Discovery begins its journey up the Missouri River.
August 12, 1805	The team sets out for home.
August 17, 1805	The main party arrives at the Shoshone camp, where Sacagawea recognizes the chief as her brother.
March 23, 1806	Lewis discovers that there is no Northwest Passage.

2. What was the most important fact learned during the Lewis and Clark Expedition?

_____

_____

3. What is the significance of the fact that only one person died during the trip?

_____

_____

4. Who initiated the expedition?

_____

5. How did Sacagawea help the expedition?

_____

_____

6. Have you ever heard of Sacagawea before? What did you hear about her? Explain.

_____

_____

Nervous System

Together, your brain and spinal cord make up your nervous system, which is the body's communication network. The most basic units of the nervous system are nerve cells, called neurons. Most neurons are too small to be seen by the human eye, but there are an unbelievable one hundred billion of them inside your head. They last a lifetime, so neurons are some of the oldest cells in your body.

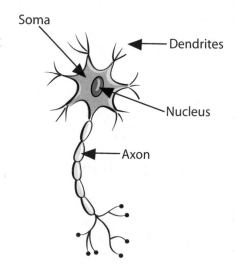

Each neuron consists of a cell body, called the soma. Out of the soma stretches a long, thin axon. The tail-like axon carries nerve impulses, which are messages, from the cell body to other neurons. Some axons are wrapped in a fatty, white substance called myelin, which protects them from damage. The myelin makes those nerves appear shiny and white, so the area of the brain that contains these nerves is called white matter.

Branching out from the body of the cell are thread-like *dendrites*, which means "tree-like." Dendrites receive messages from the axons of other neurons and transmit them to the soma. Axons and dendrites are sometimes called nerve fibers.

Neurons are surrounded by glial cells, or glia. Glia insulate and protect neurons. They also keep debris from the body away from neurons and carry nutrients to neurons.

Messages are passed from a neuron's axon to connected neurons in the form of chemicals called neurotransmitters. They flow from a message-sending neuron to a targeted neuron across a gap called a synapse. The chemicals attach to a slot, called a receptor site, on the surface of the receiving neuron.

Once attached, different neurotransmitters can instruct the message to stop or go, like a traffic light. The neurotransmitter sends signals, in the form of charged particles, that allow the message to be passed to the next neuron in the communication line, or it sends signals that prevent the message from being forwarded. A large concentration of positively-charged particles entering a receiving neuron tells it to pass on the message—it has a green light. On the other hand, a large concentration of negatively-charged particles entering the neuron will not allow it to pass on the message—it has a red light.

A single receiving neuron has thousands of receptor sites and may receive many different messages at once. Each neuron processes the incoming signals and determines whether or not to pass the information along to other cells. To avoid confusion and overload, the brain keeps tight control of this message delivery system.

Answer the questions about the reading.

1. Write *T* or *F* next to each statement from the reading to tell if it is true or false.

_____ A large concentration of negatively-charged particles entering a receiving neuron tells it to pass on the message.

_____ Most neurons are too small to be seen by the human eye, but there are an unbelievable one hundred billion of them inside your head.

_____ Once attached, different neurotransmitters can instruct the message to stop or go, like a traffic light.

_____ The chemicals attach to a slot, called a dendrite, on the surface of the receiving neuron.

2. The main purpose of the nervous system is to _____.

communicate   eat   move

3. Why does the brain have to filter messages? _____

_____

_____

4. Each neuron has a cell body, called the _____.

5. Messages are passed from one neuron to another in the form of chemicals called

_____.

6. Non-myelin neurons appear gray. What might the area of the brain that contains these neurons be called?_____

7. What does the term *dendrites* in paragraph 3 mean? Why do you think they have this name?

_____

_____

8. The word *concentration* in paragraph 6 means ____. Circle the letter of the answer.

   a. game   **b.** canine   **c.** amount

9. The word *network* in paragraph 1 refers to ____. Circle the letter of the answer.

   a. a system of channels   **b.** information   **c.** passing on a message

10. The word *transmit* in paragraph 3 means ____. Circle the letter of the answer.

   a. refuse   **b.** convey   **c.** swallow

Reading Your Mind

Modern technology allows scientists to look inside a living human brain to see what is happening. These procedures are safe and painless. By understanding normal brain activity, doctors and scientists are better able to assess the brain's behavior during times of injury, disease, and mental illness.

CT or CAT scans: Computed tomography (CT) or computerized axial tomography (CAT) show images of the brain by passing multiple X-ray beams through the brain tissue. CT or CAT scans show a cross-section of the brain, versus regular X-rays, which only show a two-dimensional view of the brain. These scans can be used to find brain tumors.

MRI scans: Magnetic resonance imaging (MRI) uses powerful magnets to cause the atoms of the brain to shake. MRI sensors pick up the signals emitted from the brain's atoms and a computer interprets them as a picture. MRIs show more detail than CT or CAT scans can. They are especially useful in finding brain tumors that grow on the back of the brain, between the ears.

PET scans: Positron emission tomography (PET) is different from other scans because it shows how the brain functions. After a person's bloodstream is injected with a small dose of glucose, which is what gives the brain energy, scanners around the head detect where the glucose moves. The PET scan shows which parts of the brain use a lot of glucose, which are the more active parts. PET scans are helpful for diagnosing strokes, studying mental illness, and learning how the brain processes language.

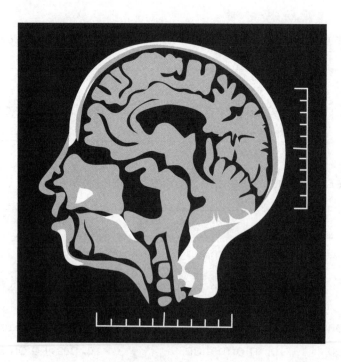

Answer the questions about the reading.

1. Match each scan to the characteristics that describe it.

uses powerful magnets to make the atoms of the brain shake

Positron Emission Tomography scan   shows a cross-section of the brain

shows how the brain functions

Magnetic Resonance Imaging scan   shows images of the brain by passing multiple X-ray beams through the brain tissue

shows which parts of the brain use a lot of glucose

Computed Axial Tomography Scan

helpful for diagnosing strokes

useful for finding brain tumors that grow on the back of the brain, between the ears

2. Modern _____ allows scientists to look inside a living human brain to see what is happening.
drugs   technology   warfare

3. Doctors and scientists are able to understand the brain's reaction to injury, disease, or mental illness by contrasting it with _____ brain activity.
altered   psychotic   normal

4. A woman is finding it difficult to understand words. What type of scan might she be given?

_____

5. A man has a lump on the base of his head. What type of scan might he be given?

_____

Plate Planet

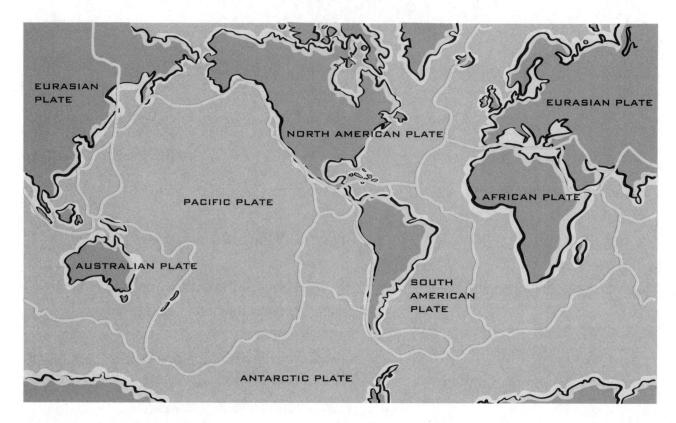

Earth is neither like a bouncy ball full of air, nor like a solid ball, such as a baseball. Earth is like an onion, with many different layers of material under its surface. But the top layer is the most fascinating.

Imagine a frozen pond, beneath which warmer, unfrozen water circulates. If you were to push something heavy across it, the ice would make a cracking sound and likely fracture. The resulting plates will be interlocked, but as melting occurs, they will have space to shift and float apart. Earth's surface is similar to the ice.

Earth's crust, or lithosphere, is broken up into huge plates that sit atop the mantle. Composed of rock, these plates drift on the surface of the planet, moving both horizontally and vertically. Earth's plates are between 50 and 250 miles thick and move between 1 and 10 centimeters per year. Over long periods of time, the plates also change in size as their margins are augmented, crushed together, or pushed back into the mantle.

The study of this amazing phenomenon is called plate tectonics, which means "plate structure." Developed in the 1960s, plate tectonics explains the movement of the earth's plates and identifies earthquakes, volcanoes, oceanic trenches, mountain range formation, and many other geologic phenomena effects of this movement.

Use the map and the reading to answer the questions.

1. What is the name of the plate on which the United States sits?

_____

2. What analogy does the author use to explain the earth's plates?

_____

3. What is the term for the earth's crust? _____

4. List three effects of plate interaction.

_____

_____

5. Which plate covers the lower part of the plate map?_____

6. What simile does the author use to describe the contents of earth?_____

_____

7. How many different plates are shown on the map? _____

8. Which of the effects mentioned do you think might happen if two plates slowly collided?

_____

9. The word *augmented* in paragraph 3 means_____. Circle the letter of the answer.
   a. deleted   **b.** formed   **c.** increased

10. Which of the effects mentioned do you think might happen if two plates scraped against each other?

_____

Moving Plates

Earth's plates can interact in various ways, and each causes a different type of deformation.

Divergent Plate Movement

Seafloor spreading is the movement of two oceanic plates away from each other, along a divergent plate boundary. This results in the formation of new oceanic crust along a mid-ocean ridge.

Lateral Slipping Plate Movement

Two plates moving against each other in opposite directions at a transform plate boundary causes a tremendous amount of friction, which makes the movement jerky. The plates slip past each other, but then stick again, while friction and pressure build up. Suddenly this pressure is released as the plates quickly jerk apart, causing an earthquake.

Convergent Plate Movement

When two plates collide at a convergent plate boundary, some crust is destroyed in the impact, decreasing the size of the plates.

If an oceanic plate and continental plate collide, the oceanic plate is forced under the continental plate in a phenomenon called subduction. If two oceanic plates collide, one may be pushed under the other and magma from the mantle rises, forming volcanoes.

If two continental plates collide, the colliding crust is compressed and pushed upward. This results in the formation of mountain ranges.

Answer the questions about the reading.

1. Match each type of plate movement to the geologic phenomenon or phenomena it causes.

Divergent Plate Movement

Convergent Plate Movement

Lateral Slipping Plate Movement

mountain range formation
volcano formation
earthquakes
ocean crust formation
subduction

2. What do you think *deformation* means? Write the letter of the answer on the line. ____
   a. same thing
   b. something that formed backward
   c. alteration of form or shape

3. What is an antonym for the word *compressed*? _____
   expanded   pressed   squeezed

4. Based on the descriptions in the reading, label the following diagrams to indicate what type of plate movement they depict.

a. _____   **b.** _____   **c.** _____

5. Which type of plate movement could form Mt. St. Helens? _____

6. Which type of plate movement could form the Ring of Fire? _____

7. Which type of plate movement could form the Mid-Atlantic Ridge? _____

8. Which type of plate movement could form the San Andreas Fault? _____

Alfred Wegener

Alfred Wegener was a German geologist, meteorologist, and explorer. He is probably best known for developing the theory of continental drift. His book *The Origin of Continents and Oceans* contains extended accounts of his ideas on continental drift, and is the basis for the well-established theory of plate tectonics.

Wegener was born in Berlin, Germany, in 1880. From an early age, he was very interested in Greenland. He walked, skated, and hiked as though training for an expedition. These exercises would indeed help him on his many Greenland expeditions as an adult, during which he measured the ice there.

Wegener studied in Germany and Austria, receiving his Ph.D. in astronomy. But he quickly dropped astronomy to study meteorology, the new science of weather. He experimented with kites and balloons, and in 1906 he even set a world record in an international balloon contest. That same year, he made his first expedition to Greenland as the official meteorologist on a Danish expedition. When he returned, he began teaching meteorology at the University of Marburg.

In 1910, Wegener noticed something unusual about the coastlines of the Atlantic continents: they looked like they had once fit together, like pieces of a puzzle that had been separated. He spoke about this idea of "continental displacement" in January of 1912. The idea would later become known as continental drift.

He published his ideas in 1915 in his book, *The Origin of Continents and Oceans*. Wegener claimed that the continents had separated into the landmasses we know today. Wegener hypothesized that there was an original, gigantic "supercontinent" that existed about 200 million years ago. He named the super continent *Pangaea*, meaning "All-earth." Pangaea was a supercontinent consisting of all of the earth's landmasses. It existed from the Permian until the Jurassic period. During the Jurassic period, Pangaea began breaking apart into two smaller supercontinents called Laurasia and Gondwanaland, and later these broke into our modern-day continents. His ideas supported and gave credibility to the theories of continental drift and plate tectonics.

Wegener's ideas were radically different from the accepted beliefs of the time. This led to some backlash, with some scientists supporting Wegener, while other scientists opposed him, including his own father-in-law!

Answer the questions about the reading.

1. Alfred Wegener was crazy for suggesting that Pangaea existed. *Fact* or *opinion*?

_____

2. Alfred Wegener published his ideas in 1915 in his book, *The Origin of Continents and Oceans*.
Fact or *opinion*? _____

3. Alfred Wegener noticed the occurrence of continental displacement. *Fact* or *opinion*?

_____

4. Alfred Wegener's parents should not have let him study Greenland, hike, or explore.
Fact or *opinion*? _____

5. What country did Wegener seem fascinated about? _____
What makes you think so?

_____

_____

6. After obtaining a high academic degree in astronomy, what other science did Wegener pursue?

_____

7. What does this tell you about Alfred Wegener?

_____

_____

8. What is Pangaea?

_____

_____

9. Why do you think it got its name?

_____

_____

10. Read the last paragraph again. How do you think Wegener felt about these reactions?

_____

_____

Mixing Metaphors

As you read the story, fill in each blank with any word from the correct part of speech. Have fun!

My mother once told me that a _____ in the hand is worth two in the bush.
NOUN

But I always thought that the _____ bird gets the worm. She also warned me not to
ADJECTIVE

put all my _____ in one basket. All the while, my father persuaded me that I should
PLURAL NOUN

_____ while the iron is hot, but at the same time, I should look before I
VERB

_____. Grandmother reminded me that I made my bed and so I'd have to
VERB

_____ in it. Grandfather also told me that a _____ and his money
VERB   NOUN

are soon parted. What were they talking about? I was so confused!

A proverb is a popular saying that expresses simple wisdom, usually through metaphor. Use your knowledge of proverbs to rewrite the story so that it makes sense.

My mother once told me that a _____ in the hand is worth two in the bush.
NOUN

But I always thought that the _____ bird gets the worm. She also warned me not to
ADJECTIVE

put all my _____ in one basket. All the while, my father persuaded me that I should
PLURAL NOUN

_____ while the iron is hot, but at the same time, I should look before I
VERB

_____. Grandmother reminded me that I made my bed and so I'd have to
VERB

_____ in it. Grandfather also told me that a _____ and his money
VERB   NOUN

are soon parted. What were they talking about? I was so confused!

1. Which phrase means "those who get rich, but are not wise with their money, will soon be poor again"?

_____

_____

2. Which phrase means "arriving early allows one to acquire the prize"?

_____

_____

3. Which phrase means "one should be careful of making hasty decisions"?

_____

_____

4. Which phrase means "if you create a situation, you have to deal with the repercussions of it"?

_____

_____

5. Can you think of other proverbs? List them here.

_____

_____

_____

_____

_____

_____

Underground Railroad

Contrary to its name, the Underground Railroad was not an actual railroad. Rather, it was a vast network of people working secretly to help fugitive slaves escape north and to Canada. Sometimes called the Freedom Trail, this network of escape routes operated for many years before and during the Civil War.

Hundreds of slaves moved north to freedom each year via the Underground Railroad. Escape routes stretched from the southern slave states into the free northern states and up to Canada. Escaped slaves were considered fugitives of the law, so they traveled secretly—usually at night, with the Northern Star as their guide—and were hidden along their route in safe houses, barns, and haylofts.

Some form of organized system to assist runaway slaves probably began in the 1780s under Quaker sponsorship. In 1786, George Washington is said to have complained about a "society of Quakers" helping one of his runaway slaves. This system of slave-helping people continued to grow, and in 1831 it was given the nickname "the Underground Railroad," after the steam railroads that were emerging at the time. Other railroad terms were used in regards to the network of people helping slaves: A "conductor" was a person responsible for moving fugitives from one place to the next; homes and businesses where fugitives would rest and eat were called "stations" and "depots" that were run by "stationmasters"; and people who contributed money or goods were called "stockholders."

Most of the people helping the fugitive slaves were antislavery blacks, but many whites also supported the Underground Railroad. The highest number of slaves escaped from the upper South, because of its close proximity to the free states. These slaves were most often single, young males, as only rarely would an entire family of slaves attempt to make an escape together.

Escaping to freedom was an arduous task. First, a slave had to escape from the slaveholder. Sometimes a "conductor" posing as a slave would enter a plantation and then guide the runaway out. The fugitive would sometimes travel between 10 and 20 miles to the next station, where they would rest and eat, hiding in barns and other out-of-the-way places. While the slave waited, a message would be sent to the next station to alert its stationmaster. Border points, such as Cincinnati, Ohio, and Wilmington, Delaware, and lake ports of Detroit, Michigan; Sandusky, Ohio; Erie, Pennsylvania; and Buffalo, New York, were all popular escape terminals, where conductors would meet the slaves and help them to freedom.

Vigilance groups sprang up in many northern areas, including New York, Philadelphia, and Boston. These were groups of people who offered support to the fugitives in the form of money, food, and lodging. They also helped these former slaves settle into a community by finding them jobs and providing letters of recommendation.

The Underground Railroad included many notable participants, including John Fairfield, who made many daring rescues; Levi Coffin, a Quaker who assisted more than 3,000 slaves; and Harriet Tubman, who made 19 trips into the South and shepherded more than 300 slaves to freedom. Thousands of antislavery campaigners, both black and white, risked their lives to operate the railway.

Answer the questions about the reading.

1. What was the Underground Railroad?

_____

_____

2. When did it operate?

_____

3. How would you describe slaves who escaped to travel the Underground Railroad?

_____

4. How would you describe the "conductors" and others who helped the slaves?

_____

5. How would you describe vigilance groups?

_____

6. Name two famous participants in the Underground Railroad.

_____

7. Could a train travel the Underground Railroad? Explain.

_____

_____

8. Who first started an organized system to help slaves escape?

_____

9. What famous American does the reading mention to have owned slaves?

_____

10. List three popular escape terminals.

_____

_____

_____

Harriet Tubman

Perhaps the most well-known Underground Railroad "conductor" is Harriet Tubman. During the course of ten years, this former slave made 19 trips into the South and ushered more than 300 slaves to freedom.

Harriet Tubman was born in Maryland around 1820. She was born Araminta Ross, but later changed her first name to Harriet, after her mother. As a small child, she worked as a house servant, and as an adolescent she worked in the fields. Around 1844, she married a free black named John Tubman and took his last name. By 1849, Tubman began to fear that she and the other slaves on the plantation would be sold.

So Tubman resolved to run away, and she began her journey one night on foot. She made her way to Pennsylvania by using the Northern Star as a guide. In the city of Philadelphia, she found work and saved her money. Soon afterward, Tubman made a dangerous trip back south to Maryland and from there escorted her sister and her sister's children to freedom, too. Then, she made a second trip to the South to rescue her brother and two other men.

On her third trip to the South, Harriet intended to escort her husband to safety in the North, but when she arrived, she learned that he had taken another wife. Harriet remained undeterred. She found other slaves seeking freedom and escorted them instead to the North. Tubman even rescued her 70-year-old parents.

Time and time again, Harriet Tubman returned to the South, seeking more slaves to help. To continue to do this undetected, she had to devise some clever strategies. For example, she would leave on a Saturday night because runaway notices couldn't be placed in newspapers until Monday morning. If she encountered people whom she thought were slave-hunters, she would turn around and pretend to be heading South. Tubman carried a gun on her journeys. If a fugitive slave became too tired or felt afraid and wanted to turn back, Tubman would actually threaten the slave, telling him or her, "You'll be free or die."

By 1856, Tubman was a wanted woman. Pro-slavery authorities were looking for her, and a $40,000 reward was offered for her capture. Harriet Tubman endured more hardship and peril than nearly anyone else in history in order to assist enslaved people. She was even dubbed "Moses."

After the Civil War, Harriet Tubman settled in Auburn, New York, where she died in 1913. During her life, she was a slave, a fugitive, and worked for the Union as a cook, a nurse, and a spy. And in all her journeys rescuing slaves from the South along the Underground Railroad, she said that she "never lost a single passenger."

Use the clues to complete the crossword puzzle about the reading.

Across

1. Harriet Tubman could be described as this kind of person.

2. Harriet Tubman was one of these on the Underground Railroad.

3. Harriet Tubman escaped because she was afraid of being this.

4. Harriet Tubman's nickname.

Down

5. Harriet Tubman escaped to this state.

6. Harriet Tubman's journeys can be described as this.

7. Harriet Tubman was born as one of these.

8. Harriet Tubman settled in this state.

9. Harriet Tubman would use this to persuade tired slaves to persist.

10. On Harriet Tubman's first trip back to the South, she saved this relative.

Diary of a Slave

Dear Diary,
My whole life I've been a slave on this plantation in Maryland. I work day in and day out, making this white farmer rich. I don't know the taste of freedom. But I do know that slavery tastes bitter. Tomorrow, I make my escape, for I hear that a better existence awaits me in the North.
Henrietta

1

Dear Diary,
Last night I stole away with my brother Thomas. With every step I took my fear grew higher in my throat, but then we met Moses, of whom I've heard tales from the other slaves. The lot of us quietly passed across the bridge on the Choptank River and headed toward Delaware. Many hours later, we stopped at a house with a lantern on its hitching post. Moses told us this was a safe place, so Thomas tapped on the door. I thought I'd stop breathing, for I feared the worst: that maybe it was all a trap. That we'd be caught and beaten, or worse—sent back to slavery. But some kindly folks shuffled us inside their warm home. They gave us food and showed us a secret door with a dug-out space behind it. We curled up inside for a long overdue rest, being sure to stay silent. As I drifted off, I was still gripped with fear of being caught.
Henrietta

2

Dear Diary,
It has been many weeks since my last entry. After leaving Wilmington, Delaware, Thomas and I endured a trek that lasted for hundreds of miles. Every day we grew more tired and hungry, and the only thing that kept us going was the thought that there would be freedom at the end of the journey. We crossed through the Appalachian Mountains to Rochester. A kindly white woman named Susan fed us and gave us warm clothes, for the weather grows cool up here in the North. Tomorrow, we move on toward Canada—the only place where we can truly be free.
Henrietta

3

Dear Diary,
Yesterday, we boarded a ferryboat and traveled across Lake Erie. I am astonished at the generosity of the people in the North, especially these white folks that have been helping us. They are breaking the law just as much as we are, and yet they risk everything to help a common Negro slave. I will forever be indebted, for today, I am a free woman.
Henrietta

4

Answer the questions about the diary entries.

1. Who is writing this diary, and how would you describe her?

_____

_____

2. How does the author feel about her life in the first entry?

_____

_____

3. How does she feel during the second entry?

_____

_____

4. How does she feel by the last entry?

_____

_____

5. Describe her journey in a few adjectives.

_____

_____

6. Who is Moses?

_____

7. Who do you think Susan might be?

_____

8. What does a lantern on a hitching post mean?

_____

9. Where does the author begin her journey, and where does she end up?

_____

10. If you were the author of this diary, would you have done the same thing? Explain.

_____

_____

_____

A Southern Plantation

Imagine that you are the son or daughter of a wealthy Southern slave owner. Your father wants you to take over the plantation, but you oppose slavery. What will you do? Write a story about it.

_____

_____

_____

_____

_____

_____

_____

_____

_____

_____

_____

_____

_____

_____

A Helping Hand?

Imagine that you are an antislavery Northerner. One night, fugitive slaves arrive on your doorstep. What happens next? Write a story about it.

_____

_____

_____

_____

_____

_____

_____

_____

_____

_____

_____

_____

_____

_____

_____

_____

_____

_____

_____

Soul Food

The term *soul food* is now commonly used to describe a style of food that originated during a dark time in the history of the United States. The soul food we know today was developed by African slaves who were being held in the South. This cuisine was fashioned from the meager ingredients available to the slave and sharecropper families.

The slave ships transporting Africans to the United States were also filled with African crops with which to feed the "cargo." These crops included rice, okra, yams, peanuts, and black-eyed peas. Over time, these and other African foods, grains, and spices helped fashion a form of southern cuisine.

Much of the food consumed by slaves used the extra ingredients of meals they prepared for whites or whatever else they could grow or catch on their own to supplement the rations their owners doled out to them. The enslaved took leftover or discarded animal parts—such as pig's feet and ham hocks—and employed African cooking techniques and homegrown vegetables and spices to create tasty dishes.

Africans who regularly cooked meals for their owners introduced their special cuisine to white planters and farmers. African cooks may have introduced deep fat frying, a common African cooking technique for preserving chicken and beef. The African custom of roasting pigs, beef, chickens, and lambs on an open spit with a pan of sauce on the side for dipping the meat may have been the origins of the Southern barbecue.

Another important African dish popular in the South was *fufu*, a type of pancake prepared by boiling water and stirring in flour and other ingredients. Cornbread was prepared by enslaved Africans, and was similar to African millet bread. Slaves boiled the hulled and dried kernels of Indian corn, or hominy, and ground them into a meal known as grits to make a food similar to the African dish called *eba*. Today, Southerners eat grits regularly.

Over time, these foods became a basic component of Southern cuisine. While the origins of soul food aren't pleasant, the result was a special blending of African and American culinary styles, producing food that is vibrant and rich in character.

Answer the questions about the reading.

1. Number these events in the correct order.
   _____ African slaves were given meager ingredients, so they developed their own style of food.
   _____ Africans were brought from Africa, along with African ingredients.
   _____ The African slave style of cooking became popular and is now called soul food.

2. How does the author feel about slavery in the United States?
   _____

3. How does the author express this? Underline the sentences that tell you.

4. In what region of the country did soul food originate? _____

5. What were some of the unique ingredients that were carried from Africa?
   _____
   _____

6. What is one method of food preparation that the slaves used?
   _____

7. What is *fufu*?
   _____

8. What is *hominy*?
   _____

9. How would you describe the food rationed to the slaves by their owners? Circle all that apply.

meager	abundant	plentiful	scanty	scraps
leftovers	enviable	copious	paramount	measly
paltry	undesirable	discarded	lavish	

10. Have you ever eaten soul food? What is your favorite dish?
   _____
   _____

Southern Biscuits

Buttermilk Biscuits

2 cups flour

$1\frac{1}{4}$ teaspoons baking powder

$\frac{1}{2}$ teaspoon baking soda

1 teaspoon salt

10 tablespoons shortening

1 cup buttermilk

Preheat oven to 450 degrees. Sift together flour, baking powder, baking soda, and salt into a large bowl. Work in the shortening with fingertips until the mixture is like coarse meal. Beat in the buttermilk until a stiff dough is formed. Knead dough in bowl for 1 minute. Roll the dough out on a lightly floured board until about $\frac{1}{2}$-inch thick and cut out 12 to 14 rounds. Place biscuits on a baking sheet. Bake 12 minutes or until nicely brown. Serve hot.

Cheese Biscuits

2 cups self-rising flour

1 teaspoon baking powder

1 teaspoon sugar

$\frac{1}{3}$ cup shortening

$\frac{3}{4}$ cup grated cheddar cheese

1 cup buttermilk

Preheat oven to 350 degrees. Mix flour, baking powder, and sugar using a fork; cut in shortening until it resembles cornmeal. Add cheese. Pour in buttermilk and stir just until blended. Do not overstir. Use a tablespoon or ice cream scoop to drop portions on a well-greased baking sheet. Bake for 12 to 15 minutes.

Compare and contrast the biscuit recipes. Write a *P* next to the statements that refer to plain buttermilk biscuits, a *C* next to those about cheese biscuits, or a *B* only to those about both.

1. These contain buttermilk. ____

2. These contain cheddar cheese. ____

3. These require kneading. ____

4. These call for self-rising flour. ____

5. These bake at 450 degrees. ____

6. These should be rolled out. ____

7. These bake for 12 minutes or so. ____

8. These contain salt. ____

9. What do you think might happen if you overstirred the cheese biscuit mixture?

_____

_____

10. What do you think might happen if you rolled the buttermilk biscuit dough to be one inch thick?

_____

_____

Changing the Civil War

Originally, the American Civil War was fought by the North to prevent the secession of the Southern states from the Union. Conflicts over slavery had been a major cause of the war, but abolishing slavery was not in fact a goal of the war. However, that changed when President Abraham Lincoln issued his Preliminary Emancipation Proclamation on September 22, 1862. The Emancipation Proclamation is now viewed as a milestone in the path to ending slavery.

The Emancipation Proclamation stated that as of January 1, 1863, "all persons held as slaves" within the rebellious areas "are, and henceforward shall be free." This was a bold step on the part of Lincoln to change the goals of the war. He hoped to inspire all blacks, and in particular, slaves in the Confederacy, to support the Union cause and to keep England and France from giving political recognition and military aid to the Confederacy.

The Emancipation Proclamation was merely a military measure, which limited its power in many ways. It applied only to states that had seceded from the Union, which excluded the loyal border states, which held slaves, too. The Emancipation Proclamation also exempted parts of the Confederacy that had already come under Union control. Another key element of the Proclamation was that the freedom it promised depended upon Union military victory.

The Emancipation Proclamation did announce the acceptance of black men into the Union Army and Navy, thus enabling the freed slaves to become liberators themselves. By the end of the war, almost 200,000 black soldiers and sailors had fought for the Union. The Emancipation Proclamation confirmed that the Civil War was now a war for freedom. It boosted the morale of the Union cause and strengthened the Union both militarily and politically.

Though the Emancipation Proclamation did not end slavery in the nation, it did deeply transform the spirit of the Civil War. The Emancipation Proclamation has assumed a place among the great documents of human freedom.

Answer the questions about the reading.

1. What is the main idea of this reading?

_____

_____

2. What does the word *secession* in paragraph 1 mean?

_____

3. What was perhaps the most significant change that the Emancipation Proclamation effected?

_____

_____

4. If you were a slave at the time, how do you think this document would have made you feel?

_____

5. Who issued the Emancipation Proclamation?

_____

6. List two limitations of the Emancipation Proclamation.

_____

_____

7. How many black soldiers fought for the Union? _____

8. Why was it significant that the Emancipation enabled freed slaves to become liberators themselves?

_____

_____

9. What was President Lincoln hoping to accomplish with the Emancipation Proclamation?

_____

_____

10. What does the word *exempted* in paragraph 3 mean?

_____

Emancipation Proclamation

Emancipation Proclamation

Whereas on the 22nd day of September, A.D. 1862, a proclamation was issued by the President of the United States, containing, among other things, the following, to wit:

That on the 1st day of January, A.D. 1863, all persons held as slaves within any State or designated part of a State the people whereof shall then be in rebellion against the United States shall be then, thenceforward, and forever free; and the executive government of the United States, including the military and naval authority thereof, will recognize and maintain the freedom of such persons and will do no act or acts to repress such persons, or any of them, in any efforts they may make for their actual freedom.

That the executive will on the 1st day of January aforesaid, by proclamation, designate the States and parts of States, if any, in which the people thereof, respectively, shall then be in rebellion against the United States; and the fact that any State or the people thereof shall on that day be in good faith represented in the Congress of the United States by members chosen thereto at elections wherein a majority of the qualified voters of such States shall have participated shall, in the absence of strong countervailing testimony, be deemed conclusive evidence that such State and the people thereof are not then in rebellion against the United States."

Now, therefore, I, Abraham Lincoln, President of the United States, by virtue of the power in me vested as Commander-In-Chief of the Army and Navy of the United States in time of actual armed rebellion against the authority and government of the United States, and as a fit and necessary war measure for supressing said rebellion, do, on this 1st day of January, A.D. 1863, and in accordance with my purpose so to do, publicly proclaimed for the full period of one hundred days from the first day above mentioned, order and designate as the States and parts of States wherein the people thereof, respectively, are this day in rebellion against the United States the following, to wit:

Arkansas, Texas, Louisiana (except the parishes of St. Bernard, Palquemines, Jefferson, St. John, St. Charles, St. James, Ascension, Assumption, Terrebone, Lafourche, St. Mary, St. Martin, and Orleans, including the city of New Orleans), Mississippi, Alabama, Florida, Georgia, South Carolina, North Carolina, and Virginia (except the forty-eight counties designated as West Virginia, and also the counties of Berkeley, Accomac, Northhampton, Elizabeth City, York, Princess Anne, and Norfolk, including the cities of Norfolk and Portsmouth), and which excepted parts are for the present left precisely as if this proclamation were not issued.

And by virtue of the power and for the purpose aforesaid, I do order and declare that all persons held as slaves within said designated States and parts of States are, and henceforward shall be, free; and that the Executive Government of the United States, including the military and naval authorities thereof, will recognize and maintain the freedom of said persons.

And I hereby enjoin upon the people so declared to be free to abstain from all violence, unless in necessary self-defense; and I recommend to them that, in all cases when allowed, they labor faithfully for reasonable wages.

And I further declare and make known that such persons of suitable condition will be received into the armed service of the United States to garrison forts, positions, stations, and other places, and to man vessels of all sorts in said service.

And upon this act, sincerely believed to be an act of justice, warranted by the Constitution upon military necessity, I invoke the considerate judgment of mankind and the gracious favor of Almighty God.

Answer the questions about the document.

1. What type of source is this? _____

tertiary   secondary   primary

2. Why might this type of source be more useful than other types?

_____

_____

3. When was this document issued?

_____

4. Why does the document list specific places?

_____

_____

5. What power allowed Lincoln to issue this document? Underline the part that tells you.

6. How do you think slaves reacted to this document?

_____

7. How do you think those who were pro-slavery reacted to this document?

_____

8. What cited document does Lincoln feel makes his Proclamation warranted?

_____

9. What does Lincoln recommend that freed persons do? Underline the part that tells you.

10. What does *A.D.* mean, and when is it used?

_____

_____

_____

School Days

1432 Deerhead Road
Swallowstown, PA 84765

Mr. Mario Lasky
Superintendent of Schools
Swallowstown School District
49 Hinton Road
Swallowstown, PA 84765

March 21, 2009

Dear Mr. Lasky:

I feel that lengthening the current school day would be detrimental to the student body. There would be much less time for after-school activities, which are enjoyable, educational, and help keep children out of trouble after school. But if the school day were made longer, clubs and organizations would suffer. Many children wouldn't be able to stay at school even later than they do now. Some parents might not want their children returning from school late in the day, and students may not have a way to get home if the current schedule changes. In addition, outdoor sports teams would suffer because they would not have enough time to practice before dark.

Another reason that the school day should not be made longer is because it would allow students less time to do assignments and study. Returning home from school later would mean that students have less time to do homework before bedtime. Students need this time to practice and reinforce what they learn in school at home.

Longer school days would also mean that students would have less time to spend with family and friends. Children need to time interact with their friends to develop social skills and to maintain a strong family bond. A longer school day would prohibit this.

I feel very strongly that the Swallowstown school district should not make the school days end later than they currently do. I believe that lengthening school days will negatively affect many important aspects of a child's life: after-school programs, academics, and socialization. I intend to vocalize these thoughts at the upcoming Swallowstown school board call-to-action meetings. We must keep our children's best interests at heart in this matter.

Thank you for your time and consideration.

Sincerely,
Ms. Zoey Walker

Answer the questions about the letter.

1. To whom is this letter being written and why?

_____

_____

2. Who might Ms. Zoey Walker be?

_____

3. What opinion is being expressed in this letter?

_____

_____

4. Does the writer adequately support her opinion with reasons? Explain.

_____

_____

5. Do you agree or disagree with the writer on this issue? Why?

_____

_____

6. Do you think your response is influenced by the fact that you are a student? How so?

_____

_____

7. Circle the word that is an antonym of *detrimental*.

      damaging   harmful   beneficial

8. What does the word *educational* in paragraph 1 mean? Write the letter of the answer on the line.

_____

  a. offering knowledge   **b.** numbing the mind   **c.** detrimental

9. Underline the phrase that means the opposite of *socialize*.

    to involve oneself with one's peers

    to involve oneself in society

    to remain uninvolved

10. What does *vocalize* in paragraph 4 mean? Write the letter of the answer on the line. _____

  a. give a voice to   **b.** be silent   **c.** be mute

Rocks Tell Time

Earth's surface is constantly changing, and its rocks are evidence of past geologic events. The age of rocks can be determined in various ways. By using relative-dating principles and noting the position of layers within a rock, it is also possible to reconstruct the sequence of geologic events that have occurred at a site.

One way scientists do this is by using the principle of uniformitarianism, which states that the processes affecting the earth today are the same ones that affected it in the past. For example, at an active volcano, today, lava can be observed to cool and form layers of basalt. Therefore, any time one sees layers of basalt, it can be assumed that they likely formed from lava cooling after a volcanic eruption.

Second, the principle of original horizontality states that most sedimentary rock is deposited in a horizontal position, which means they form layers. The principle of superposition can be used to interpret the relative ages of these layers: In a sequence of undisturbed sedimentary layers or lava flows, the oldest layers are at the bottom. These principles allow scientists to determine the relative age of a rock compared with another rock. They can also compare the ages of rock layers in different areas. This type of comparison has enabled them to create a list of earth's rock layers from youngest to oldest, called a geologic column.

Another way to test a rock's age is by using radioactivity. Radioactive parts of elements in rocks decay into other elements at a constant pace called a half-life. By comparing the amount of the original element with the amount present today, scientists can come up with an absolute age for a rock. These ages are compiled into a history of earth. Long stretches of time on earth are called eras. Earth's rock history includes the Paleozoic, Mesozoic, and Cenozoic eras.

The scientists who interpret the stories told by rocks are called structural geologists and stratigraphers. Structural geologists carefully observe and interpret layers of rock. They study the way in which earth's crust is deformed by mountain-building processes. They also study clues at the earth's surface that reveal the underlying structure and geologic history of an area. Stratigraphers compare vertical sequences of rock layers from different areas to piece together the geologic history of a region.

Answer the questions about the reading.

1. Explain what uniformitarianism means.

_____

_____

2. Explain what structural geologists do.

_____

_____

_____

3. Place a check next to the phrase that best describes the author's purpose.

_____ to instruct   _____ to inform   _____ to entertain

4. A stratigrapher might compare the layers of rock in the Grand Canyon in Arizona and the layers of rock in Bryce Canyon in Utah to determine that they both experienced some of the same episodes of erosion and deposition. *True* or *false*? _____

5. A stratigrapher might study the way earth's crust has been deformed by the formation of the Himalayas. *True* or *false*? _____

6. Another way to test a rock's age is by using radioactivity. *True* or *false*? _____

7. A list of earth's rock layers from oldest to youngest is called a geologic column. *True* or *false*?

_____

8. Earth's rock history includes the Jurassic, Cretaceous, and Tertiary eras. *True* or *false*?

_____

9. Gray horizontal layers of limestone are exposed in the desert. Which layers do you think are the oldest?

_____

10. Layers of basalt are found in Mexico. How do you think they formed?

_____

Geologic Column

Like rocks, the history of life forms can be shown as a geologic column.

PERIOD		EXAMPLE OF LIFE FORM
CENOZOIC ERA (2-65 Millions of Years Ago)		
Tertiary		Primitive Horses
MESOZOIC ERA (65-245 Millions of Years Ago)		
Cretaceous		Last Dinosaurs
Jurassic		Quarry Dinosaurs
Triassic		First Dinosaurs
PALEOZOIC ERA (245-570 Millions of Years Ago)		
Permian		Primitive Reptiles
Pennsylvanian		Giant Insects
Mississippian		Brachiopods
Devonian		Primitive Fishes
Silurian		Sea Scorpions
Ordovician		Nautiloids
Cambrian		Trilobites

Answer the questions using the chart.

1. Using the knowledge you gained from the previous reading, what is this geologic column?

_____

_____

2. In this chart, which era is most recent?

_____

3. Why might the chart not extend beyond Cambrian?

_____

_____

4. What animal is pictured in the Pennsylvanian Period?

_____

5. The remains of a triceratops are found. From what era is this creature?

_____

Match each era to its period and/or life form. Match all that apply.

Paleozoic   Cretaceous Period

                                                   primitive reptiles

                                                   Devonian Period

Mesozoic   Tertiary Period

                                                   primitive horses

                                                   sea scorpion

Cenozoic   Permian Period

                                                   quarry dinosaurs

Naming Dinosaurs

Richard Owen was an English anatomist, zoologist, and vertebrate paleontologist. Owen was the most distinguished zoologist in Britain during the mid-19th century and is responsible for coining the term *dinosauria*.

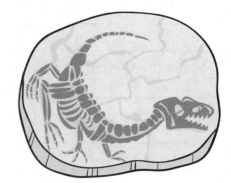

Owen was born in Lancaster, England, and earned a degree from the University of Edinburgh in Scotland. Owen was a principal founder of London's British Museum, which is now the Natural History Museum. He served as superintendent of the natural history collections at the museum from 1856 until his retirement in 1883.

Owen was also appointed at the Royal College of Surgeons. During this time in his career, Owen took the opportunity to dissect the animals that died in the Regent's Park Zoological Gardens in London. This new knowledge of animal anatomy served him well when he began to examine the fossil bones of extinct vertebrates, which were then being found in increasing numbers in southern England and on the European continent.

In 1841, Owen formulated the first classification of the creatures that he named the *Dinosauria*, recognizing them as a suborder of large, extinct reptiles. The word *dinosauria* comes from the Greek words *deinos*, meaning "fearfully great," and *sauros*, meaning "lizard."

Owen had noticed that a group of fossils had certain characteristics in common, including column-like legs—versus the sprawling legs that other reptiles have—and five vertebrae fused both to one another and to the pelvic girdle. In 1842, Owen proposed this new name in an article published in the *Proceedings of the British Association for the Advancement of Science*. In his article, Owen explained, "The combination of such characters, some, as it were, from groups now distinct from each other, and all manifested by creatures far surpassing in size the largest of existing reptiles, will, it is presumed, be deemed sufficient ground for establishing a distinct tribe or suborder of Saurian Reptiles, for which I would propose the name of Dinosauria."

Throughout the course of his life, Owen produced 625 publications, which encompassed the anatomy of living invertebrate and vertebrate animals as well as of a large range of extinct organisms, including the dodo of Mauritius, the moas of New Zealand, the giant ground sloths of Argentina, and the marsupials of Australia. He designed the first constructions of dinosaurs, which were exhibited at the Crystal Palace in London. In all, Richard Owen left a rich legacy of scientific discoveries.

Circle the answers to the clues in the word puzzle below.

1. animals with backbones

2. one who specializes in anatomy

3. the term Richard Owen coined

4. the country in which Richard Owen was born

5. thing preserved from a past geologic age

6. one who studies the branch of biology concerned with the classification and the characteristics of animals

7. the type of animal that dinosaurs are

8. to separate into pieces

9. a member of the order of mammals that usually have a pouch on the abdomen of the female which serves to carry the young

10. no longer in existence

M	A	R	S	U	P	I	A	L	V	E	Q	C	Z
D	O	E	G	D	I	S	S	E	C	T	E	G	O
C	E	N	G	L	A	N	D	E	C	U	Z	U	O
A	X	N	A	C	A	F	I	F	O	S	S	I	L
Q	T	S	N	C	D	V	N	E	H	R	K	G	O
F	I	Y	A	E	Q	U	O	U	E	E	T	Y	G
E	N	L	T	S	O	L	S	T	F	P	N	K	I
C	C	V	O	S	N	O	A	G	M	T	S	E	S
T	T	A	M	F	C	H	U	Z	G	I	N	A	T
U	B	N	I	U	O	A	R	V	D	L	V	A	E
D	T	I	S	L	A	V	I	E	Q	E	E	L	R
V	E	R	T	E	B	R	A	T	E	S	T	O	C

63

Dinosaur Mistakes

Many misconceptions circulate about the life and times of the dinosaurs.

Myth 1: The term *dinosaur* means "terrible lizard."

Reality Check: Richard Owen originally defined the term to mean "fearfully-great lizard." The word is derived from the Greek language. Scientists now know that the dinosaurs were neither terrible nor lizards.

Myth 2: Dinosaurs and humans coexisted.

Reality Check: Not even close! The death of the last dinosaur and the appearance of the first human were separated by about 62 million years.

Myth 3: The latest dinosaur books and films are true.

Reality Check: Not so much. Professional dinosaur paleontologists do not review most dinosaur books and scripts for accuracy. That means they are often erroneous or outdated, and may reflect the personal bias of the writer.

Myth 4: Mammals ate dinosaur eggs, contributing to the dinosaurs' extinction.

Reality Check: Mammals and dinosaurs indeed coexisted in the late Triassic Period. However, there is no evidence that dinosaurs became extinct because of predation on their eggs.

Myth 5: An asteroid or comet killed the dinosaurs.

Reality Check: Well, maybe. The cause of the dinosaur extinction is a controversy that continues among paleontologists. However, evidence from a deep-sea core drilled off the coast of Florida proves that an asteroid hit the earth at the end of the Cretaceous Period, which likely caused the dinosaur extinction. Most dinosaur specialists are willing to accept that an asteroid hit the earth, but some do not think that it was the sole cause of the Mesozoic extinctions. Instead, they claim that dinosaurian diversity was already in decline by the end of the Cretaceous Period. The asteroid impact may have been the straw that broke the camel's back.

Myth 6: All large, monster-like reptiles from prehistoric times were dinosaurs.

Reality Check: Dinosaurs represented less than 10% of the 40 groups of reptiles from the Mesozoic Era. Pterodactyls, sea-serpents, giant lizards, pelycosaurs, and other big prehistoric beasts were not in fact dinosaurs.

Myth 7: Archaeologists dig up dinosaurs.
Reality Check: Nope! Archaeology, which is a subdivision of anthropology, deals only with humans and covers just the last 3–4 million years. Paleontology, which is a combination of geology and biology, deals with all fossils and covers the last 3.5 billion years.

Myth 8: All the dinosaurs lived and died during the same period of time.
Reality Check: Dinosaurs were around for a very, very long time. The distance in time between Tyrannosaurus and Apatosaurus is about 65 million years.

Myth 9: Dinosaurs were all hot-blooded or all cold-blooded.
Reality Check: Neither are true! Mesozoic dinosaurs were not warm-blooded like modern mammals, nor were they cold-blooded like modern lizards. Most specialists believe that dinosaurs were dinosaur-blooded, a condition that combines certain aspects of warm-bloodedness with a changing metabolism over the animal's lifetime.

Myth 10: Dinosaurs represent extinction, and therefore, failure.
Reality Check: Negative! Dinosaurs are actually the best examples of success and adaptation. They ruled the earth longer than any other land animals: more than 150 million years! They also gave rise to birds.

Answer the questions about the dinosaur myths.

1. Have you ever heard any of these myths before and believed them? Which ones?
_____
_____

2. What type of blood did dinosaurs have? _____

_____

3. What killed off the dinosaurs? Explain. _____

_____

_____

4. How long were dinosaurs around? _____

5. What do you think the word *predation* in myth 4 means?

_____

6. What do you think the word *bias* in myth 3 means? Write the letter of the answer. ____
    a. prejudice   **b.** fair   **c.** just

7. "The straw that broke the camel's back" is what type of phrase?

_____

Jurassic Park Reality Check

Modern filmmakers often ponder the possibility of bringing back the dinosaurs, and what the repercussions would be. Sadly, dinosaurs are extinct, and by definition, they are permanently gone. Here are the reasons why returning them to earth remains an impossible feat of science.

For starters, scientists would need to find DNA of the species, and find it completely intact. The problem with DNA is that it degrades over time. After several million years, many pieces of the DNA would be lost. Gaps in a DNA strand cannot be repaired, so the information is lost forever. It's not possible simply to improvise the genetic code of an organism.

Even if the intact DNA could be found in something that preserves DNA well, such as amber, it would have to be extracted. One would be lucky to get even a few pieces of intact DNA extracted, and it would be certainly impossible to remove the whole genetic code of the dinosaur. Even if the DNA were inside an insect, for example, it would be an enormous challenge to remove the dinosaur DNA unmixed with the insect's DNA.

However, presuming that it could indeed be obtained, the DNA would then have to be sequenced to uncover the genetic code of the dinosaur. A genetic code consists of several billion letters strung together in a chain, and one gap in the chain could possibly ruin the whole thing. If scientists somehow acquired an entire, intact dinosaur genetic code, they would next need to assemble it into chromosomes, which they simply don't know how to do with dinosaur DNA. This process could take decades to untangle.

Another major hindrance to recreating dinosaurs is the fact that the chromosomes must then be implanted into a compatible, living, intact egg. In vertebrates, the same species' or a closely related species' egg and cytoplasm are required for the egg to develop normally. Crocodile eggs, or even eggs of the same dinosaur genus, would not work, and we certainly don't have a living dinosaur egg lying around.

Even if scientists could create this fairy-tale egg, the egg would have to be "raised" under the optimal conditions for that species' development. But scientists don't know what those conditions might be. If the baby dinosaur managed to hatch, it would have to be kept alive in a world full of germs and other dangers to which it would have no resistance. The world has changed a lot in 65 million years. So it seems that receiving a pet Triceratops probably won't happen for your next birthday!

Answer the questions about the reading.

1. Number the steps to make a hypothetical dinosaur.

_____ Assemble DNA into chromosomes.

_____ Find complete, intact DNA of the species.

_____ Keep baby dinosaur alive in a world full of germs and other dangers to which it would have no resistance.

_____ "Raise" egg under the optimal conditions for that species' development.

_____ Implant chromosomes into a compatible, living, intact egg.

_____ Extract DNA from its source.

_____ Sequence DNA to uncover the genetic code of the dinosaur.

2. Can you think of any movies, television programs, or books in which dinosaurs are brought back to life? Name them.

_____

3. Do you think this could really happen?

_____

4. Would you like to have a pet Triceratops? Explain.

_____

_____

5. What is the primary reason that dinosaurs cannot be recreated?

_____

Moral Question

Imagine that science can allow the dinosaurs to be brought back to life. Consider the ethics of applying revolutionary scientific technologies. Do you approve of this radical idea? Explain.

_____

_____

_____

_____

_____

_____

_____

_____

_____

_____

_____

_____

Moving Out

Imagine that dinosaurs have taken over the earth. Humans must relocate to another planet in order to survive. In a letter to the governing body of that planet, pose that the human race be allowed to live there.

_____

_____

_____

_____

_____

_____

_____

_____

_____

_____

_____

_____

_____

_____

Your Own Jurassic Park

Write a proposal for your own dinosaur theme park, in which dinosaurs have been brought back to life and are kept on display at the park, much like the feature film *Jurassic Park*. If necessary, finish on a separate sheet of paper. Consider the following:

What types of materials would you need?
What types of dinosaurs would you raise?
How would you maintain the park and control the crowds?
How would you raise the necessary funds to create and
      support the park?
What types of staff members would need to be hired?
Also consider potential problems, such as:
      What would you do if dinosaurs escaped?
      What would you do if a patron were hurt by a dinosaur?
      How would you keep the dinosaurs inside the park?

_____

_____

_____

_____

_____

_____

_____

_____

_____

_____

_____

_____

In the space provided, draw a layout of the park, like the map of a zoo or theme park.

Dinosaur Superlatives

MOST LIKELY TO HAVE PLATES FOR PROTECTION

ANKYLOSAURUS

MOST LIKELY TO HAVE FIERCE CLAWS

DEINOCHEIRUS

MOST LIKELY TO IMPERSONATE A BIRD

UNENLAGIA

MOST LIKELY TO HAVE A HUGE HEAD

PENTACERATOPS

MOST LIKELY TO HAVE PLENTY OF TEETH

HADROSAURUS

MOST LIKELY TO HAVE THE LARGEST EGGS

HYSELOSAURUS

MOST LIKELY TO OUTLIVE MOST OF US

SAUROPOD

MOST LIKELY TO HAVE THE LONGEST TAIL

DIPLODOCUS

MOST LIKELY TO HAVE THE SHORTEST NAME

MINMI   **KHAAN**

MOST LIKELY TO HAVE THE LONGEST NAME

MICROPACHYCEPHALOSAURUS

MOST LIKELY TO KILL ANYTHING IN ITS PATH

MEGARAPTOR

DEINONYCHUS   **UTAHRAPTOR**

Answer the questions about the reading.

1. Which dinosaur would you least want to meet? _____

2. Which dinosaur name would perhaps be the funniest name for a human baby?
   _____

3. You want to make the largest hard-boiled egg ever. Which dino's unfertilized egg would you use?
   _____

4. Enemies are hurling things toward you. What dino should you send out to investigate?
   _____

5. Which dino is a dentist's favorite?_____

6. You are designing a one-size-fits-all helmet for dinosaurs. Which dino might be a problem to fit?
   _____

7. Which dino would you least want to be in a boxing match with?
   _____

8. Which dinosaurs would be easy to call?
   _____

9. Which dino is a bird that can't fly?
   _____

10. Which dinosaur would have been around for a while?
    _____

California Gold Rush

The California Gold Rush was the massive movement of people to California after the discovery of gold there in 1848. The California Gold Rush became one of the most significant events in the state's history for several reasons, including: People came from around the world and stayed there, forming the multicultural heart of California that still exists; and America was pulled westward, ensuring that California and other parts of the West would become a part of the United States.

A carpenter named James W. Marshall first discovered gold in California in January 1848. In partnership with John A. Sutter, Marshall was working to build a sawmill on the American River in California's Sacramento Valley. Within a few months' time, a full-scale rush to get gold was set off by a shrewd local merchant named Samuel Brannan, who hoped to increase his business. One of the early Mormon settlers in San Francisco, Brannan owned a store near Sutter's fort and his idea was to make a lot of money by taking advantage of news of gold in the area. So in May of 1848, he returned to San Francisco and spread the word of gold. Brannan literally ran down the streets of San Francisco shouting to get people's attention. Within a few days, the onslaught began.

Boats filled with people from San Francisco headed up the Sacramento River to look for gold. Foreseeing this reaction, Brannan had stocked his store with mining supplies, and his business was thriving. By that summer, the news spread up and down the West Coast, across the border to Mexico, the Mississippi Valley, and the Eastern states.

People from all walks of life set out for California in search of the American Dream, an ideal in which anyone who seeks prosperity can find it. Many pawned their possessions to pay for travel from countries all over the world, including Mexico, China, Germany, France, Turkey, and Australia. The gold-seekers were also known as "49ers" because most headed to California in 1849. In fact, California still has a football team that boasts the name 49ers, named after these entrepreneurs.

Several common routes were used to access California during the gold rush, including an overland route on the Oregon-California Trail. Regardless of the route, the travel was an intensely difficult journey. Many of these gold-seekers found what they had come for, at least at first. At the beginning of the gold rush, gold was relatively easy to find, but the enterprise became quickly difficult as it yielded less and less. Those who did find gold usually didn't gain extreme wealth from it, but rather, ended up spending it all on the basic necessities of life. The biggest moneymakers were the opportunistic entrepreneurs who supplied the gold miners with much-needed supplies and services, the way Samuel Brannan did. While the California hills eventually ran dry of gold, the impact of the gold rush lives on.

Answer the questions about the reading.

1. Who first discovered gold in California? Write the letter of the answer. ____
   a. James Polk   **b.** John Sutter   **c.** Sam Brannan   **d.** James Marshall

2. Where was gold in California first found? Write the letter of the answer. ____
   a. American River   **b.** Los Angeles   **c.** San Francisco   **d.** Donner Pass

3. The American River is likely closest to what major city? Write the letter of the answer. ____
   a. San Francisco   **b.** Sacramento   **c.** Oakland   **d.** Los Angeles

4. What is an entrepreneur?
   _____

5. What are two definitions of a 49er?
   _____
   _____

6. What was the American Dream?
   _____
   _____

7. What does the word *opportunistic* in the last paragraph mean?
   _____
   _____

8. Sam Brannan ran down the streets of San Francisco and shouted to get people's attention. How do promoters get our attention today?
   _____
   _____

9. Sam Brannan promoted the gold rush by creating hype around it. Can you think of events in modern life that are over-promoted or "hyped" by the media?
   _____
   _____

10. When did the California Gold Rush begin? _____

Routes to the Gold

Those seeking gold in California during the gold rush of the 1800s often faced an immediate problem: California was a long way from home. At this time, travel was not exactly quick and easy. There was no railroad, bus, or airplane to whisk people to California.

The two primary choices of transportation were by land or by sea, and this decision forced travelers to pick the better of two evils. The sea route around the tip of South America often lasted more than six months. But the alternative was a 2,000-mile trek across the barren American outback. Either way, the journey would be a test of endurance.

Those from the East Coast favored traveling to California by sea. However, the long route around South America was nearly intolerable. The food along the journey was often rancid or bug-ridden. Water stored for months in a ship's hold was almost impossible to drink. And seasickness was rampant.

Seeking a faster, more direct route, others tried taking a ship to the Isthmus of Panama, then trekking overland to the Pacific side. Keep in mind that there was no Panama Canal at the time. At the Pacific coast, the gold-seekers would wait for another ship to pick them up—hopefully. They sometimes waited there weeks or even months for another ship. When a ship finally did arrive, passage might cost $500 or $1,000—an extraordinary amount of money at the time. And, sometimes there was no space, even if a traveler had the funds. To add insult to injury, many of the ships on the Pacific side of the voyage were not sea worthy and sank en route.

For many people, the overland route across America was the only possible way to go. It was much shorter than the sea route, but it wasn't faster. Fortune-seekers plodded westward alongside covered wagons at two miles per hour. This journey could take them six months. They encountered Native Americans for the first time, whom they feared, although their real fear should have been water, or lack thereof.

Many of those journeying didn't prepare well enough for the trip, and water was either spoiled or in short supply. Price-gouging became a problem, with the cost of water going as high as $100.00 per drink. Those without money, and therefore water, were sometimes left to die. It was a lesson in supply and demand that they learned the hard way.

One inventive California-bound man named Rufus Porter actually tried to create an aircraft to take people to the gold. Porter planned to fly people west on propeller-driven balloons powered by steam engines. He went as far as posting advertisements and even managed to sign up 200 people for the trip. But the contraption never lifted off the ground. Clearly, everyone was in a big hurry to get west, so they could strike gold!

Answer the questions about the reading.

1. What is meant by "the better of two evils"? _____
   _____

2. Figure out how many steps it took to walk all the way to California. First, measure in inches one of your normal steps from the heel of your front foot to the heel of your back foot. Next, divide 63,360 (the number of inches in a mile) by that number. Now you have figured the number of steps in a mile. Now, multiply the number of steps by 2,000 miles, the distance to California from Missouri. Write here the number of steps it would take for you to walk to California!
   _____

3. Why did ships have to go around South America to get to California?
   _____

4. What were two problems for travelers who opted to cut across Panama over land?
   _____
   _____

5. Imagine that you travel back in time and become a gold-seeker. You are allowed to take along one modern invention that will fit in your pocket. What would you take and why?
   _____
   _____

6. What were two problems faced by travelers who opted to take the Oregon-California Trail?
   _____
   _____

7. What was Rufus Porter's idea? Did it work?
   _____

8. If you had to spend six months on a ship or in a wagon, how do you think you would feel?
   _____
   _____

9. "When a ship finally did arrive, passage might cost $500 or $1,000—an extraordinary amount of money at the time." What financial concept does this sentence illustrate?
   _____

10. Before the gold rush, a metal pan in California cost 30 cents, but after gold was discovered, the same pan sold for $15.00. The price change was a result of the economic laws of supply and demand. Can you think of items today that are more expensive because they are in short supply?
    _____
    _____

Along the Oregon Trail

Most of the 49ers coming from the Midwest or East Coast decided to travel the overland route on the Oregon-California Trail. For many, travel by ship was too costly an option. Maps and books of the time seemed to promise a quick and easy voyage across the country. But for the people who traveled overland, the journey would be grueling and many would not survive it.

Those seeking riches in California experienced a vast variety of circumstances that they had never before encountered. Many were in covered wagons, many rode horses, and still many others simply walked the distance. Once outside of established frontier towns, they were in wilderness. Many were citygoers who had never camped outdoors, hunted for food, or built a fire. And now they faced months far from the conveniences of civilization.

Enduring the weather was another major struggle. They braved violent thunderstorms and torrential rain that turned the land into a massive mud hole. They also suffered through scorching heat. Sunblock lotion had not been invented yet, so those who survived the journey suffered from dry, sun-baked skin for months.

To say that the travel conditions were unsanitary would be an understatement. Hundreds died along the overland trail in the quest for monetary freedom. They sweated profusely through 90-degree heat, were covered in dust and dirt kicked up with each step, and they could rarely change their clothes or bathe themselves. They often had no choice but to drink rancid water, which resulted inevitably in stomach illness.

Many imagined that they would follow a lone wagon or two across the country, but in reality, the trip was crowded! Packs of wagons would pass each day, causing wagon "traffic," and crowding was a problem, especially at night when the wagons congregated at camp. Many discovered that previous wagon trains had overgrazed the prairie, so there was no remaining grass for the oxen and mules to eat. Thousands of animals died from exhaustion or thirst and were left to rot in the sun.

Further, each new wagon train dug its latrine near previous ones, and so the waste often leaked into the water supply. Such conditions helped make disease the most prevalent killer of 49ers, who fell victim to cholera, mountain fever, pneumonia, and diphtheria.

Some would find their fortunes. Most would not. But they had survived their overland journey by a combination of bravery, cooperation, skill, and luck. The experience had changed them forever.

Answer the questions about the reading.

1. Why was traveling the Oregon-California Trail to California the only option for many 49ers?

_____

2. How did the 49ers travel this route?

_____

_____

3. What problems did the weather present for the 49ers?

_____

_____

4. What killed more 49ers than anything else?

_____

5. How would you describe the cleanliness on the Oregon-California Trail?_____

hygienic   sterile   unsanitary

6. To understand what life was like for the 49ers, try an evening without any modern conveniences: no electric lights, microwave ovens, computer, TV, and anything else that needs electricity. Make a complete list of all the things you give up.

_____

_____

7. How was life without these conveniences? Explain.

_____

_____

8. How did the animals fare on the trip west? Circle all that apply.

exhausted   rejuvenated   exhilarated

thirsty   sated   famished

9. Underline an antonym of *rancid*.

stale   fresh   rotten

10. Was there traffic along the trail? Explain.

_____

_____

Striking Gold

This map shows some of the important mines of the California Gold Rush.

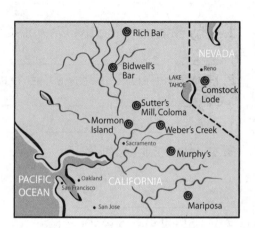

Place: Sutter's Mill/Coloma
Date of gold discovery: January 24, 1848
The California Gold Rush began when James Marshall spotted bits of gold in the American River. The news brought thousands of prospectors to the area. Ironically, neither Marshall nor his employer John Sutter prospered from the find.

Place: Mormon Island
Date of gold discovery: February 1848
Mormons working for John Sutter made a gold find a few miles up the American River.

Place: Bidwell's Bar
Date of gold discovery: July 4, 1848
Another of John Sutter's employees, John Bidwell, made a strike farther north, in an area that became known as Bidwell's Bar. The land was so rich with gold that one miner later built a mansion with his profits and still had enough gold left to bury $100,000 ($2.4 million today) of it for safekeeping.

Place: Weber's Creek
Date of gold discovery: summer 1848
One gold claim in this area resulted in $17,000 ($415,000 today) worth of gold in a single week.

Place: Murphy's
Date of gold discovery: 1848
The Murphy brothers struck gold just a few days after arriving in the Sierras; by the end of the year, they had $1.5 million worth ($37 million today).

Place: Mariposa
Date of gold discovery: 1849
This immensely lucrative property at the southern edge of the gold fields belonged to a man named John Fremont. His Mexican workers regularly sent him buckskin bags filled with 100 pounds of gold.

Place: Rich Bar
Date of gold discovery: 1850
Three German miners made an enormous find in the northern section of the gold fields. Rich Bar would produce $23 million of gold ($561 million today).

Place: Comstock Lode
Date of gold discovery: 1859
The discovery of silver on the other side of the Sierras in Nevada brought an end to the California Gold Rush; at its height, though, about $80 million (around $1.9 billion today) had been pulled annually from the gold fields. However, that figure had fallen by almost half when the Comstock Lode was discovered.

Answer the questions about the reading.

1. Match each place to the time in which gold was found there.

Sutter's Mill/Coloma	February 1848
Comstock Lode	July 4, 1848
Bidwell's Bar	1850
Rich Bar	1859
Mormon Island	January 24, 1848
Weber's Creek	Summer 1848

2. What border state is shown on this map? _____

3. Can you name a famous glittering city located in that state in modern times?

_____

4. Why are the dollar amounts translated to modern amounts in this reading? For example, "$80 million (about $1.9 billion in 2005 dollars)".

_____

5. From what continent did the miners at Rich Bar come? _____

_____

6. In 1848, how much was 37 million dollars worth? _____

_____

7. From previous knowledge, do you know who the Mormons are?

_____

8. Why do you think that the amount of gold being mined had fallen by almost half when Comstock Lode was discovered?

_____

Packing List

Many of the 49ers left home in Missouri for a 2,000-mile journey to California. Some walked the entire distance on foot! If you were planning to journey 2,000 miles across the wilderness, what would you take along? Remember, there are no supply points along the way; you must pack everything you need to last three months. Make a list of your supplies.

_____

_____

_____

_____

_____

_____

_____

_____

_____

_____

_____

Map It Out

Before they left for California, the 49ers plotted their route west. With this modern map of the United States, plot a route from Florida to Sacramento. Try to find the fastest route, keeping in mind that mountain ranges, rivers, and climate will all have a huge impact on your journey.

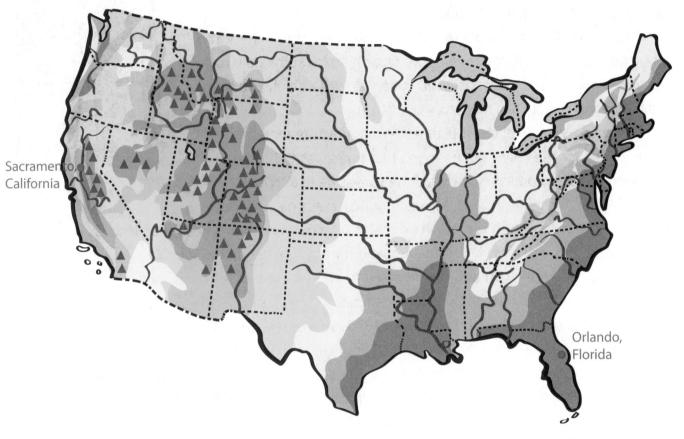

Now write a short paragraph explaining why you chose that route.

_____

_____

_____

_____

_____

_____

_____

_____

Miners' Jeans

The blue jean is undoubtedly the most American article of clothing that exists. And no wonder: They were born out of the American Dream. Bavarian immigrant Levi Strauss invented blue jeans in the mid-19th century as miners' pants. Strauss is one of the best-known beneficiaries of California's gold-rush economic boom.

In the 1850s, 24-year-old Levi Strauss had been living in New York, but he relocated to California with hopes of cashing in on the gold rush. He opened a store that sold supplies to miners as well as high-end linens to the growing city of San Francisco.

Trained as a tailor, Strauss planned to manufacture tents and wagon covers for the 49ers. But he found that there wasn't much of a market for these products, so he used the canvas he had to make remarkably durable pants instead. Miners found Strauss's pants perfect for their line of work, which was harsh on their clothing. Word soon spread that Strauss's pants could survive a miner's tough lifestyle and the demand for them grew quickly. Soon Strauss was selling his practical, robust pants as fast as he could make them.

Strauss eventually began using blue denim (called *genes* in French, which became *jeans* in English) to make some of his pants. Then, in 1872, Strauss received a letter from Nevada tailor Jacob Davis, in which Davis detailed the way he made pants for his customers. He explained to Strauss that he placed metal rivets at the points of strain on pants, such as at pocket corners and the base of the fly. Davis didn't have the money to patent this process, so he suggested that Strauss and he take out the patent together. The patent was granted in 1873, and jeans as we know them today were born!

The first blue jeans came in two styles: indigo blue and brown cotton duck. By the 1900s, Strauss's blue jeans, which were originally entirely practical, were embraced by the fashion industry. They even appeared in *Vogue* magazine in 1935. Since then, America has had a love affair with jeans. Levi Strauss's invention has become an international phenomenon and an icon of American culture.

Needless to say, Strauss made a fortune on his miners' pants turned blue jeans. In fact, Strauss's company remains one of the nation's leading apparel manufacturers.

Answer the questions about the reading.

1. What caused Levi Strauss to move from New York to California?

_____

2. What was the ultimate effect of this move?

_____

3. Do you think that Strauss expected this level of success? Why or why not?

_____

_____

4. For whom were Levi Strauss's pants originally intended? _____

5. Who wears them now? _____

6. What is the origin of the word *jeans*?

_____

7. Who came up with the idea of adding rivets to jeans?

_____

8. How did Strauss end up with them on the pants he produced?

_____

_____

9. What is the significance of Strauss's pants today?

_____

_____

10. Do you own a pair of jeans? Did you have any idea that they were originally meant for work, and not as a fashionable item of clothing?

_____

Endangered Everglades

𝕱𝖑𝖔𝖗𝖎𝖉𝖆 𝕿𝖎𝖒𝖊𝖘-𝕳𝖊𝖗𝖆𝖑𝖉 𝕽𝖊𝖈𝖔𝖗𝖉

March 2, 2009

OP-ED

The negative impact of mankind on other species is extremely evident in south Florida's Everglades region. Man's desire for land and raw materials, continued pollution, and indiscriminate hunting has placed many plant and wildlife species on the edge of extinction.

Within the four National Park areas of Everglades National Park, Biscayne National Park, Big Cypress National Preserve, and Fort Jefferson National Monument, there are 16 endangered and 6 threatened wildlife species. Here are just a few:

American crocodile (*Crocodylus acutus*)

Green turtle (*Chelonia mydas*)

Atlantic Ridley turtle (*Lepidochelys kempi*)

Atlantic leatherback turtle (*Dermochelys coriacea*)

Cape Sable seaside sparrow (*Ammodramus maritima mirabilis*)

Wood stork (*Mycteria americana*)

West Indian manatee (*Trichechus manatus*)

Florida panther (*Felis concolor coryi*)

Key Largo cotton mouse (*Peromyscus gossypinus allapaticola*)

Red-cockaded woodpecker (*Picoides borealis*)

Schaus swallowtail butterfly (*Papilio aristodemus ponceanus*)

But what is being done, if anything? Only the answer is that some measures are being taken, but they still aren't enough. For the last decade, the South Florida Research Center has been studying how changes occurring outside the parks affect the delicate areas within their boundaries. This type of research may lead to a brighter future for many species. Legislation such as the Endangered Species Act of 1973 has also afforded some measure of protection for wildlife. The act provides for the classification of wildlife species as "endangered" or "threatened," and authorizes legal protection of species listed.

Public support is also vital for species preservation. As a private citizen, you can become informed on the status of plants and wildlife in Florida and support conservation legislation. You can also be proactive by opting not to purchase products derived from endangered or threatened plant or wildlife species. Furthermore, you should report to authorities those who are known dealers of endangered or threatened plants and wildlife.

Answer the questions about the article.

1. From what type of publication is this article?

_____

2. What do you think Op-Ed stands for?

_____

3. Place a check next to the reason why the author might have written this article.

_____ as a how-to

_____ to persuade

_____ to entertain

4. How do you think the author feels about humans' effect on the Everglades?

_____

_____

5. Underline the words in the first paragraph that help express this.

6. Why does the author pose a question?

_____

7. What answers does the author offer to this question?

_____

_____

_____

8. What does the author suggest that others do?

_____

_____

_____

9. What does the word *preservation* in the last paragraph mean?

_____

10. What does the noun *effect* mean? What does the verb *affect* mean?

_____

_____

Everglades Habitats

The Everglades National Park is often characterized as a water marsh, but in reality, it consists of several distinct habitats. Slight changes in elevation, salinity, and soil throughout this park have resulted in different environments, each with its own community of plants and animals.

Mangroves

In the coastal channels and winding rivers of the Everglades area, majestic mangrove forests are found. Red mangroves and black-and-white mangroves thrive in tidal waters, where freshwater mixes with saltwater. Mangrove forests are a valuable nursery for shrimp and fish. During dry months, wading birds congregate here to feed while many other bird species nest in the trees themselves.

Coastal Prairie

The coastal prairie is an arid region periodically flooded by hurricane waves and buffeted by heavy winds. It is situated between dry land and the tidal mud flats of Florida Bay. Characterizing the coastal prairie are succulents and other low-growing desert plants that can withstand the harsh conditions.

Marine/Estuarine

Florida Bay contains more than 800 square miles of marine bottom. Much of this habitat is covered by sea grass, which shelters fish and shellfish and sustains the food chain that supports all higher vertebrates in the bay. The hard bottom areas house corals and sponges.

Freshwater Slough

The slough is the deep center of a broad marshy river. The slough moves faster than other areas, but at a pace of only 100 feet per day. Sloughs are peppered with tree-islands, or hammocks. The Everglades contain two individual sloughs: Shark River Slough and Taylor Slough. There are no surface connections between the two. A series of other sloughs through the Big Cypress Swamp supply freshwater to western Florida Bay and the Ten Thousand Islands.

Freshwater Marl Prairie

Bordering deeper sloughs are large prairies, which contain marl sediment, a hard, calcium-containing material that settles on the limestone. Marl allows slow seepage of the water, but does not allow drainage. Freshwater marl prairies look a lot like freshwater sloughs.

Cypress

The cypress tree is a deciduous conifer that can survive in standing water. These trees often form dense clusters in natural water-filled depressions.

Hardwood Hammocks

Hammocks are dense stands of hardwood trees. They grow in places where the land naturally rises— only a few inches—within the Everglades. They resemble teardrop-shaped islands and are shaped by the flow of water in the middle of the slough. The tall trees provide shade in which ferns and airplants thrive inside the hammock.

Pinelands

This dry, rugged terrain sits on top of a limestone ridge. They contain primarily slash pines that take root in any crack or crevice where soil collects in the jagged bedrock. The pinelands are the most diverse habitat in the Everglades. They consist of slash pine forest, an understory of saw palmettos, and more than 200 varieties of tropical plants.

Answer the questions about the reading.

1. Match each habitat to the life that grows there.

pinelands	shrimp
hardwood hammocks	sponges
mangroves	saw palmettos
marine/estuarine	ferns
coastal prairie	succulents

2. How many different habitats are described in the reading? _____

3. Why do the Everglades have so many distinct environments?

_____

_____

4. If you were going shrimping, in which environment should you look?

_____

5. You want to see the largest variety of life in the Everglades. In which habitat should you look?

_____

6. Which two habitats look the same?

_____

Father of the Everglades

Ernest F. Coe is known as the Father of the Everglades because the national park was created through his passion and efforts. Coe was born in New Haven, Connecticut, in 1866. When Coe was a young boy, he loved to spend time outside, and as an adult, he started to explore the Everglades area. He was appalled to learn that the area's rare birds were being killed and unusual orchids were being removed from their natural habitat. Coe worried that much of the wildlife would face extinction if something wasn't done to stop the pillaging of the area.

In 1928, Coe wrote a letter to Stephen T. Mather, the first Director of the National Park Service. In his letter, Coe outlined a proposal for a national park in the lower everglades of south Florida. Coe insisted that Florida save its incomparable tropical beauty.

A meeting held to discuss the idea resulted in legislation to create Everglades National Park. Senator Duncan B. Fletcher of Florida introduced this legislation in December 1928. By May 25, 1934, it was approved, and President F. D. Roosevelt signed it five days later. While another thirteen years were needed to acquire the land and define the boundaries of the new park, Coe's dream was ultimately realized. President Harry Truman dedicated the park in 1947.

Coe had persistently and almost single-handedly pushed for the establishment of the park in the Everglades. After his death in 1951, Secretary of the Interior Oscar Chapman said of Coe, "Ernest Coe's many years of effective and unselfish efforts to save the Everglades earned him a place among the immortals of the National Park movement." Coe's efforts have been further recognized in recent times. On December 6, 1996, Everglades National Park christened its new visitor center as the Ernest F. Coe Visitor Center. This honors the man who dedicated his life to the preservation of the Everglades.

Circle the answers to the clues in the word puzzle below.

1. Ernest Coe's nickname, excluding the word *the*

2. word meaning "plunder ruthlessly"

3. Floridian flower

4. what the everglades became, thanks to Coe

5. President who approved the Everglades as a National Park

6. from your knowledge of the Everglades, a large, endangered reptile

7. word meaning "exempt from death"

8. President who dedicated the Everglades as a National Park

9. from your knowledge of the Everglades, a large, endangered mammal

10. word meaning "a matter under consideration by a legislative body"

A	M	E	R	I	C	A	N	C	R	O	C	O	D	I	L	E	L
R	O	E	G	D	I	S	S	E	C	T	E	G	O	F	D	S	E
O	E	N	A	T	I	O	N	A	L	P	A	R	K	X	M	W	G
O	X	N	A	C	A	F	I	F	O	S	S	I	L	O	C	Z	I
S	F	L	O	R	I	D	A	P	A	N	T	H	E	R	L	J	S
E	I	M	M	O	R	T	A	L	E	E	R	Y	G	M	D	P	L
V	N	L	T	S	O	L	S	T	F	P	U	K	I	F	O	I	A
E	C	V	O	S	N	O	A	G	M	T	M	E	S	S	R	L	T
L	T	A	M	F	C	H	U	Z	G	I	A	A	T	J	C	L	I
T	B	N	I	U	O	A	R	G	D	L	N	A	E	C	H	A	O
D	T	I	S	L	A	V	I	E	Q	E	E	L	R	S	I	G	N
F	A	T	H	E	R	O	F	E	V	E	R	G	L	A	D	E	S

Florida Gators

Floridians share their state with a massive reptile: the American alligator. American alligators can be found from the coastal swamps of North Carolina all the way down to the tip of southern Florida, and then west along the Gulf Coast to the mouth of the Rio Grande. Alligators usually reside in freshwater lakes, rivers, and swamps, but they can occasionally be found in brackish water.

Alligators eat a wide variety of food including crabs, fish, frogs, wading birds, raccoons, otters, deer, and other alligators. If prey is small, it may be swallowed whole. Otherwise, the gator will bite down on it repeatedly. Using a combination of sharp teeth and tremendously strong jaw muscles, it breaks bones or shells so that the whole prey can be swallowed. Large prey may also be shaken vigorously and slapped against the water or shore to rip off pieces small enough to swallow. Alligators roll underwater with very large prey, submerging the victim and drowning it. The dead prey is dragged around or guarded for several days until the meat rots enough to be ripped apart.

The Everglades are swarming with alligators, and needless to say, you don't want to have a close encounter with one of these creatures. One misconception is that alligators have poor eyesight, and this myth results in people venturing much too close. In reality, alligators have rather keen eyesight, which is an important adaptation for hunting; they are able to see and sense movement of potential prey animals. The eyes of an alligator sit nearly on each side of their heads, which gives them a wide sight range. The only place they cannot see is right behind them.

Another myth about alligators is that you should run in a zigzag pattern to escape one that is chasing you. The truth is that alligators can run up to 30 miles per hour for short distances. If an alligator does make an aggressive charge toward you, you should run fast and straight away from the alligator. Most importantly, keep going! They usually will not run very far to chase you.

Many people mistake alligators for poor climbers because of their low proximity to the ground. Alligators have sharp claws and powerful tails to help them push their bodies up. Young alligators are agile climbers and adults have been known to climb fences to get to water or escape captivity. That means that fences should be more than $4\frac{1}{2}$ feet tall to keep people and pets out of harm's way.

Speaking of pets, alligators are not good ones! While keeping an alligator as a pet may seem like a novel idea, it is dangerous to do so. Alligators are not domesticated creatures, and they will bite the hand that feeds them. Alligators are purely instinctual hunters, so they will not show affection. It is also illegal to possess or take an alligator without the proper licenses and permits from the Florida Fish and Wildlife Conservation Commission.

Answer the questions about the reading.

1. Alligators are found only in oceans. *True* or *false*? _____

2. Alligators cannot hop fences. *True* or *false*? _____

3. It is illegal to possess or take an alligator without the proper licenses and permits from the Florida Fish and Wildlife Conservation Commission. *True* or *false*? _____

4. Alligators roll underwater with very large prey, submerging the victim and drowning it. *True* or *false*? _____

5. You accidentally disturb an alligator's nest and the mother moves aggressively toward you. What should you do?

_____

_____

6. You spot an alligator on a golf course. It is right near your ball, but you've heard that it won't be able to see the ball or you. Should you retrieve the ball? Why or why not?

_____

7. An American alligator is likely to eat _____.

you   birds   elephants

8. You see an alligator on the other side of a highway wall that is up to your waist. Is it safe to stay there and observe it?

_____

_____

9. A friend shows you the baby alligator he has in the bathtub. Is keeping the alligator as a pet a good idea? Why or why not?

_____

10. What type of animals are alligators?

_____

St. Patrick's Day

St. Patrick's Day is a celebration held annually on March 17. The holiday honors Saint Patrick, the patron saint of Ireland, on the anniversary of his death in the 5th century. It commemorates his conversion of the Irish to Christianity.

The Irish have observed St. Patrick's Day as a religious holiday for thousands of years. St. Patrick's Day often falls during the Christian season of Lent, so Irish families might traditionally attend church in the morning and celebrate the holiday in the afternoon. The day can be seen as a reprieve from the sober weeks of Lent. On St. Patrick's Day, people dance, drink, and feast on the traditional meal of Irish bacon and cabbage. Adults may drink a pint of ale, a treat called "drowning the shamrock," and children may be given some candy.

Until recently, Ireland held few parades or secular celebrations on St. Patrick's Day. In fact, up until the 1970s, Irish laws mandated that pubs be closed on March 17. However, beginning in 1995, the government of Ireland established the St. Patrick's Day Festival with the goal of creating a national festival "that ranks amongst all of the greatest celebrations in the world." They saw it as an opportunity to drive tourism and showcase Ireland to the rest of the world.

The four-day festival is now held annually in Dublin and features a major parade on the 17th, as well as music and dance performances, food, crafts, and a fireworks display. The event is Ireland's largest annual celebration. Last year, close to one million people took part in Ireland's St. Patrick's Festival in Dublin.

Today, St. Patrick's Day is celebrated all over the world, including locations quite far from Ireland, such as Japan, Singapore, Russia, and Australia. North America is in fact home to the largest St. Patrick's Day productions, which are held by people of Irish descent in cities such as Chicago, New York, and Montreal.

Answer the questions about the reading.

1. Where did St. Patrick's Day originate? _____

2. Whom does the holiday celebrate?
_____

3. Where is St. Patrick's Day celebrated now? _____

4. When is St. Patrick's Day celebrated?
_____

5. Why is it held on this day?
_____

_____

6. Place a check next to what you think the word *secular* in paragraph 3 means.
_____ sacrificial
_____ adhering to religion
_____ not overtly religious

7. Place a check next to what you think the word *reprieve* in paragraph 2 means.
_____ to force to continue
_____ to give relief for a time
_____ to make a sacrifice

8. What does "drowning the shamrock" mean?
_____

_____

9. What began happening on St. Patrick's Day in Ireland in 1995?
_____

_____

10. What things do you associate with St. Patrick's Day?
_____

_____

_____

Patron Saint

Saint Patrick is the patron saint of Ireland and one of Christianity's most widely known figures. In his honor, St. Patrick's Day is popularly celebrated as a worldwide tradition. But for all his fame, the life of Saint Patrick remains somewhat of a mystery. Stories about his life have been widely exaggerated, including the famous account of his banishing all the snakes from Ireland, lending him an almost mythical quality.

Ironically, Ireland's most famous saint was actually British. Patrick was born in Britain near the end of the 4th century to the son of wealthy parents. Patrick's father was a Christian deacon, but he may have taken the role because of tax incentives, rather than out of devotion to his religion. When Patrick was sixteen years old, he went to Ireland, but not voluntarily. Patrick was taken prisoner by a group of Irish raiders who were attacking his family's estate.

The raiders brought him to Ireland, where he was held captive. There, Patrick worked as a shepherd. He often felt lonely and afraid, and thus turned to religion for comfort. After more than six years, Patrick escaped from his captors. His writings indicate that he heard a voice, which he believed to be God, that told him to leave Ireland. Patrick returned to Britain, where he experienced a second revelation in which an angel in a dream told him to return to Ireland as a missionary.

Patrick then spent more than fifteen years studying and training in religion. He became an ordained priest and was sent to Ireland with two purposes: He was to minister Christians already living in Ireland and he was to begin to convert the other Irish to Christianity. There was a small number of Christians in Ireland when Patrick arrived, but most Irish practiced a nature-based pagan religion. Their culture centered around oral legend and myth.

Patrick was familiar with the existing Irish language and culture, and so rather than aiming to eradicate these beliefs, he opted to incorporate them into his lessons of Christianity. An example of this melding of beliefs is that Patrick used bonfires to celebrate Easter because the Irish were accustomed to honoring their gods with fire.

It is believed that Patrick died on March 17, around 460 CE. And so, this is the date on which the Irish celebrate their beloved saint.

Answer the questions about the reading.

1. Who is Saint Patrick?

_____

2. Where was he born and when? Why is this ironic?

_____

3. Were his parents particularly religious? Explain.

_____

_____

4. What is Saint Patrick known for?

_____

5. What is one myth about him?

_____

6. What did you learn about traditional Irish culture from this reading?

_____

7. Number the events in the correct order.

_____ After more than six years, Patrick escaped from his captors.

_____ It is believed that Patrick died on March 17, around 460 CE.

_____ He became an ordained priest and was sent to Ireland.

_____ Patrick then spent more than fifteen years studying and training in religion.

_____ Patrick was taken prisoner by a group of Irish raiders who were attacking his family's estate.

_____ Patrick experienced a second revelation in which an angel in a dream told him to return to Ireland as a missionary.

8. What is the main idea of this reading?

_____

_____

9. What genre of literature is this reading? _____

poem   science fiction   autobiography   biography

10. Do you think that Saint Patrick respected the beliefs of the Irish? Explain.

_____

_____

_____

Irish Soda Bread

Soda bread first appeared in the 19th century, when baking soda was introduced as a leavening agent. Irish soda bread is very easy to make and has become an established favorite. A cross symbol traditionally appears on the top of loaves of Irish soda bread, but the cross is not actually a religious representation. It was simply a method of dividing the baked bread into four quarters for serving.

Ingredients:

nonstick vegetable oil spray

2 cups all-purpose flour

5 tablespoons sugar, divided

$1\frac{1}{2}$ teaspoons baking powder

1 teaspoon salt

$\frac{3}{4}$ teaspoon baking soda

3 tablespoons butter, chilled and cut into cubes

1 cup buttermilk

$\frac{2}{3}$ cup raisins

Directions:

1. Preheat oven to 375°F.
2. Spray 8-inch-diameter cake pan with nonstick spray.
3. Whisk together flour, 4 tablespoons sugar, baking powder, salt, and baking soda in a large bowl.
4. Add butter, and combine with hands into a coarse meal.
5. Make a well in center of flour mixture. Add buttermilk.
6. Gradually stir dry ingredients into milk to blend.
7. Mix in raisins.
8. Using floured hands, shape dough into ball.
9. Transfer to buttered pan and flatten slightly.
10. Sprinkle dough with remaining 1 tablespoon sugar.
11. In center of dough, cut a 4-inch cross about $\frac{1}{4}$ inch deep.
12. Bake bread until brown, about 40 minutes.
13. Cool bread in pan 10 minutes before serving.

Answer the questions about the Irish soda bread.

1. Number the steps in the correct order.

_____ Spray 8-inch-diameter cake pan with nonstick spray.

_____ Using floured hands, shape dough into ball.

_____ Cool bread in pan 10 minutes before serving.

_____ Transfer to buttered pan and flatten slightly.

_____ Whisk together flour, 4 tablespoons sugar, baking powder, salt, and baking soda in a large bowl.

2. When did soda bread first appear? _____

3. How do you think it earned its name?

_____

_____

4. Why is there a cross on top of Irish soda bread loaves?

_____

_____

5. What do you think might happen if you did not gradually stir the dry ingredients into the milk?

_____

_____

6. Circle the ingredients below that do **not** appear in this recipe.

milk	buttermilk
orange juice	eggs
butter	water
flour	raisins
lemon	sugar

Coming to America

In 1845, a monumental event called the Great Potato Famine hit Ireland. That year, a disease infected the potato crop, which was the main food source for the Irish. This caused nearly a million poor, uneducated, Catholic Irish to flee to America to escape starvation. But the Protestant majority in the United States did not warmly welcome the Irish.

Many Americans scorned the Irish for their religious beliefs and found their accents repugnant. Irish immigrants had trouble finding even the most menial jobs, and they were often faced with signs such as *No Irish Need Apply* at places of business. Another blow to the Irish was the Americans' perception of their St. Patrick's Day celebration. When the Irish took to the streets on St. Patrick's Day to celebrate their heritage, the media portrayed them in cartoons as drunk, violent monkeys.

But by the time the Civil War was near its end, the Irish realized that there was strength in numbers, and together they could use political power to their advantage. So the Irish organized. They began voting en masse, or as a whole, and their voting block, known as the "green machine," became an important swing, or deciding, vote in American politics. Suddenly, the Irish were no longer being mocked.

The annual St. Patrick's Day parades became a mandatory event for political candidates yearning for the vote of the green machine. By 1948, President Harry Truman even attended the New York City St. Patrick's Day parade. It was a proud moment for the many Irish whose ancestors had to fight stereotypes and racial prejudice to gain acceptance in America.

Then, in 1960, the Irish made another leap forward in politics: they had a Catholic president. That year, John Fitzgerald Kennedy, a famine descendant, became the thirty-fifth president of the United States. In little more than a century, Irish-Americans had moved from the position of the scorned all the way to the Oval Office.

Answer the questions about the reading.

1. What event caused the Irish to come to America in the 1800s?

_____

2. Why was this event so devastating to them?

_____

_____

3. Can you imagine being forced to flee your home country, just to survive? How do you think you would feel?

_____

_____

4. How were the Irish received in America? Why?

_____

_____

5. If you had just traveled to a new country and this happened to you, how would you feel?

_____

_____

6. What began to happen after the Civil War?

_____

_____

7. What was the "green machine"?

_____

8. Why do you think it was given this name?

_____

_____

9. What happened in 1948, and why was it significant?

_____

_____

10. What happened in 1960, and why was it significant?

_____

_____

_____

Celebrating in the Cities

Irish colonists brought St. Patrick's Day to the American colonies. The first civic and public celebration of Saint Patrick's Day in America took place in Boston, Massachusetts, in 1737. Since then, the United States has developed a reputation for commemorating the patron saint of Ireland in style.

On every St. Patrick's Day in Chicago, the locals see green. That's because the windy city has become famous for a somewhat peculiar annual event: dyeing the Chicago River green! It all began in 1961, when a city worker's coveralls were speckled with green spots. When asked how they got that way, he explained that it was dye used by city pollution-control workers to trace illegal sewage discharges. That sparked the idea to use the green dye as a unique way to celebrate St. Patrick's Day in the city of Chicago.

So, they tried it! They released 100 pounds of green vegetable dye into the river. It was overkill, however. That much dye was enough to keep it green for a week! Today, the Chicago Journeymen Plumbers still turn the Chicago River green every year for the St. Patrick's Day Parade celebration, but with less dye, of course. In order to minimize environmental damage, only forty pounds of dye are used, making the river green for only several hours. And oddly, for the first few minutes after the dye is added, the river is actually orange before it changes to the perfect shade of Irish green.

Another notable American city that celebrates St. Patrick's Day in a monumental way is New York. Each year, a massive parade marches down Manhattan's Fifth Avenue to honor the patron saint of Ireland. This New York tradition dates as far back as 1766. That was the year in which the first official parade in New York City was held. It was composed of Irishmen in a military unit recruited to serve in the American colonies. For the next few years, different military units organized the parade. But, after the war of 1811, Irish fraternal and beneficial societies took over the duties of hosting and sponsoring the event. Irish societies joined together at their respective meeting places and moved in a procession toward the famed St. Patrick's Old Cathedral, St. James Church, or one of the many other Roman Catholic churches in New York City.

However, as the years passed, individual societies merged under a single grand marshal, increasing the size of the parade. So, in 1848, several New York Irish aid societies decided to unite their parades to form just one New York City St. Patrick's Day Parade. Today, that parade is the world's oldest civilian parade and the largest in the country. Each year, about three million people line the one-and-a-half-mile parade route to watch more than 150,000 participants in the procession. This immense group takes more than five hours to travel from 44th Street and Fifth Avenue up to 86th Street.

Each year, a unit of soldiers marches at the head of the parade. The Irish 165th Infantry has become the parade's primary escort, and they are followed by the various Irish societies of the city. Some of the other major sponsors and participants in the parade include the Ancient Order of Hibernians, the thirty Irish county societies, and various Emerald, Irish-language, and Irish nationalist societies.

Answer the questions about the reading.

1. Who brought St. Patrick's Day to America?

_____

2. In what city was the first civic and public celebration of St. Patrick's Day in America?

_____

3. Match each year or number to its corresponding description.

1961	pounds of green vegetable dye released into the Chicago River the first time
1766	participants in the New York City parade procession
150,000	year in which several New York Irish aid societies decided to unite their parades to form just one New York City St. Patrick's Day Parade
1848	year in which it was realized that the Chicago River could be dyed green
100	year in which the first official parade in New York City was held

4. Would you have wanted to go swimming in the Chicago River in 1961? Explain.

_____

5. Why would the early St. Patrick's Day parades in New York have marched to churches?

_____

6. What does the word *primary* in the last paragraph mean?

_____

7. How much dye is currently used to turn the Chicago River green and why?

_____

8. How long does the effect last?

_____

9. What happens before the river turns green?

_____

10. Is there a St. Patrick's Day celebration in your town? If so, what happens?

_____

_____

_____

Symbols of a Saint

Irish culture includes a rich tradition of myths, legends, and storytelling. Tales were passed down from one generation to the next, usually orally. Over the course of time, stories were embellished, gaining fantastic details but sometimes losing their truth in the process. Many symbols are associated with St. Patrick's Day, some of which are entirely fabricated, and some of which have true roots in Saint Patrick, the missionary who brought Christianity to Ireland.

Perhaps the most commonly heard story about Saint Patrick is that during his mission in Ireland he stood on a hilltop and, with a wooden staff by his side, banished all the snakes from Ireland. This story is most certainly a myth! The banishing of the snakes was really a metaphor for the annihilation of pagan ideology from Ireland. It celebrates the fact that Saint Patrick successfully converted the Irish to Christianity. In fact, within 200 years of Patrick's first mission, Ireland was completely Christianized. Another amazing detail to note about this legend is that there is no evidence of a single snake in the Irish Isles. Also, the first written mention of this story did not appear until nearly a thousand years after Patrick's death!

The color green is a prominent symbol of St. Patrick's Day. However, the hallmark color of Saint Patrick was not actually green—it was blue! The popularity of green started in the 19th century, when green became used as a symbol for the country of Ireland. The climate of Ireland allows its landscape to be lush and green nearly all year long, earning it the nickname of the Emerald Isle. Today, wearing green is a way to pay tribute to Ireland and is thought to bring good luck. Children even play a game in which they pinch those who have forgotten to wear green on St. Patrick's Day.

The shamrock is a well-known emblem of St. Patrick's Day. The Celts called it a *seamroy*—a sacred plant in ancient Ireland. It is believed that Saint Patrick used the three-leafed shamrock to demonstrate the Christian trinity to the Irish. He explained that, just like its three leaves, the Father, Son, and Holy Spirit existed as one entity. By the 17th century, the English began to seize Irish land and make laws against the use of the Irish language and the practice of Catholicism. The Irish used their shamrock as a symbol of nationalism to demonstrate their displeasure with English rule.

Another example of Irish folklore entering the mainstream is the leprechaun. But this figure originally had nothing to do with Saint Patrick or the celebration of St. Patrick's Day. The Celtic creatures are called *lobaircin*, meaning "small-bodied fellow." Leprechauns were sort of like fairies, but cantankerous ones! The Celts believed that these little men were responsible for mending the shoes of the other fairies. They were known for their trickery and were always trying to protect their much-fabled treasure—a pot of gold. In the 1950s, the leprechaun was portrayed in a Walt Disney film as cheerful and friendly. This was a completely invented depiction, but it stuck! Now the leprechaun is an easily recognizable symbol of both St. Patrick's Day and Ireland.

Answer the questions about the reading.

1. What is a symbol?

_____

2. What is a myth?

_____

_____

3. Do any of these symbols have anything to do with Saint Patrick in reality? Explain.

_____

_____

4. What is a metaphor?

_____

_____

5. What is the political symbolism of the shamrock?

_____

_____

6. What do you learn in the first paragraph about Irish traditions?

_____

_____

7. What happens to stories as they are told over long periods of time?

_____

8. What was Saint Patrick's hallmark color? _____

9. Have you heard of any of these symbols or stories before? Which ones?

_____

_____

10. Come up with a brand-new legend about Saint Patrick and describe it here.

_____

_____

St. Patrick's Day Wishes

As you read the wishes, fill in each blank with any word from the correct part of speech. Have fun!

May your _____ outnumber the shamrocks that _____, and may
PLURAL NOUN   VERB

trouble avoid you wherever you _____.
                                                    VERB

May your _____ respect you, troubles _____ you, the angels
PLURAL NOUN   VERB

protect you, _____ and accept you.
                            PLACE

May you never forget what is worth _____ , or remember what is
                                                VERB ENDING IN -ING

_____ forgotten.
            ADVERB

May you have the _____ to know where you've _____, the insight
                              NOUN   VERB (PAST TENSE)

to know where you _____, and the foresight to know when you've gone too
                                    VERB

far.

May you have _____ words on a cold evening, a full _____ on a
                            ADJECTIVE   NOUN

_____ night, and the road downhill all the way to _____.
            ADJECTIVE   COUNTRY

May you never make a _____ when you could make a _____,
                                    NOUN   NOUN

unless you meet a _____ among your _____.
                                ANIMAL   PLURAL NOUN

May your fire be as _____ as the _____ is cold.
                                ADJECTIVE   NOUN

New Holiday

Create your own holiday! Use the space provided to describe it. Who founded it? What are its symbols? How is it celebrated? Who celebrates it? Then draw an image depicting something about your new holiday.

Banshee

Among the many fairies and spirits that are a part of Gaelic folklore, one of the most popularly known is the banshee. The banshee is a female spirit whose appearance warns a family that one of them will soon die.

According to tradition, the banshee can only appear to members of five major Irish families: the O'Neills, the O'Conners, the O'Gradys, the O'Briens, and the Kavanaghs. The banshee's appearance can vary, but she usually appears in one of three forms: a beautiful, young woman; a majestic matron; or a disheveled, old hag. The banshee appears wearing either a gray, hooded cloak or the winding sheet, or grave robe, of the dead.

Less frequently, the banshee appears to people as a washerwoman, or *bean-nighe*, and is seen washing blood-stained clothes. Supposedly, these are the clothes of the person who is about to die. The banshee may also appear in a variety of animal forms—typically ones that the Irish associate with witchcraft, such as a hooded crow, a hare, or a weasel.

Sometimes the banshee is not actually visible at all! However, she has one trademark quality: she is a very vocal spirit. Depending on the area of Ireland in which she is witnessed, the banshee can be screaming, singing, or wailing. Her sharp cries and wails are also called "keening," which is a term derived from the Irish *caoineadh*, meaning "lament." In some parts of Leinster, she is referred to as the *bean-haointe*, or keening woman, whose wail can be so piercing that it shatters glass. In Kerry, the keen is experienced more as a low, pleasant singing sound. In Tyrone, the banshee's sounds are similar to the sound of two boards being struck together.

On Rathlin Island, she sounds more like a screeching owl. As you can imagine, the phrase "screaming like a banshee" is derived from this infamous spirit.

It is also thought that banshees attend the funerals of the people whose death they lamented. She continues to wail at the services, but her voice blends in with the cries of other mourners.

Banshees have appeared to many people, including King James I of Scotland. In 1437, the king was supposedly approached by an Irish banshee who foretold his murder! There are also records of banshees attending the great houses of Ireland and the courts of local Irish kings.

Answer the questions about the reading.

1. Unscramble the words mentioned in the reading.

wlai   _____

eenk   _____

eligac   _____

folreklo   _____

pisrit   _____

dateh   _____

melant   _____

monerur   _____

2. Why might the author have written this? Write the letter of the answer. ____
   a. to persuade   **b.** as a warning   **c.** to inform

3. What is a banshee?

_____

_____

4. What do banshees look like?

_____

_____

5. What do banshees sound like?

_____

_____

6. If a banshee appeared to you, how would you feel and why?

_____

_____

7. What does *bean-nighe* mean, and what language do you think this word is from?

_____

8. What famous person reported that he saw a banshee? What significance did this have?

_____

_____

Samhain

Halloween originated as a festival called *Samhain*, which was first celebrated more than 2,000 years ago by the Celts. The word means "summer's end" and the celebration marked the end of summer and the beginning of winter. This was the end of harvest time and the beginning of a long, dark winter, a time of year that was often associated with human death.

The Celts celebrated Samhain (pronounced SOW-ihn) on the night of October 31, when they thought that the boundary between the worlds of the living and the dead became blurred. The Celts believed that the ghosts of the dead returned to visit their old homes on the night of Samhain. The ghosts would cause mischief and trouble, and damage crops. Regardless, the Celts welcomed and celebrated the ghosts.

The Celts believed that the presence of the otherworldly spirits on Samhain enhanced Celtic priests' ability to make predictions about the future. These prophecies greatly comforted the Celts, and provided them with a sense of how the long, dark winter would be.

To celebrate the holiday, the Celts lit bonfires and wore costumes typically fashioned from animal heads and skins—much more authentic versions of animal constumes worn on Halloween today! Earlier in the evening, they would have extinguished the hearth fires burning in their homes. When the celebration was over, they would reignite their hearth fires using fire from the sacred bonfire. They believed this ritual would protect them during the coming winter.

Over the course of history, other cultures conquered and affected the Celts' Samhain traditions. For example, the Romans ruled Celtic lands for more than 400 years, and combined two of their own festivals with the customary Celtic celebration of Samhain. One of these Roman festivals honored Pomona, the Roman goddess of fruit and trees. The symbol of Pomona is the apple and the incorporation of this celebration into Samhain probably explains the tradition of bobbing for apples that is practiced today on Halloween.

Later, Christianity spread into Celtic lands, and Christian leaders replaced the Celtic festival of the dead with a related, but church-sanctioned holiday called All-Hallows Eve. Eventually, it became "Halloween"!

Answer the questions about the reading.

1. Where did Halloween begin?

_____

2. What was Halloween originally called and what did it mean?

_____

3. What do Samhain and modern-day Halloween have in common?

_____

4. Who came to visit on the night of Samhain?

_____

5. What did these visitors do? Write the letter of the answer. _____
   a. cause trouble   **b.** salvage crops   **c.** bob for apples

6. Why were these visitors so important?

_____

_____

7. How would you feel if similar visitors came to visit you?

_____

_____

8. What other cultures affected Samhain over time?

_____

9. How old is Samhain?

_____

10. Why did the Celts extinguish their hearth fires on Samhain?

_____

_____

_____

The Blarney Stone

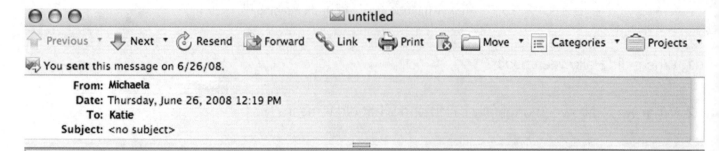

Previous ▾   Next ▾   Resend   Forward   Link ▾   Print   Move ▾   Categories ▾   Projects ▾

You **sent** this message on 6/26/08.

From: **Michaela**
Date: Thursday, June 26, 2008 12:19 PM
To: **Katie**
Subject: <no subject>

Hey Katie,

Top o' the morning to ya! I'm having a magnificent time in Ireland. We flew into Dublin and have been road-tripping around the Emerald Isle.

Today, my family and I visited Blarney Castle and its Blarney Stone, which is one of Ireland's most noted icons. It's located in the small community of Blarney, which is about six miles northwest of Cork. Cork is Ireland's second largest city, after Dublin.

I learned that the castle that stands today is the third building to have been erected on this site. The one that is there now was built in 1446 by Dermot McCarthy, King of Munster. I guess I shouldn't really say it still "stands" though. It's actually just ruins of the central keep that remain.

On the grounds is the Blarney Stone, which was a block of stone built into the battlements of the castle. I kissed it! It sounds bizarre, but it's what you're supposed to do! It's said that if you kiss the Blarney Stone, you will be forever endowed with the gift of gab. It's a tradition that dates back to Queen Elizabeth I. She intended to take possession of the castle. But whenever she discussed the matter with McCarthy, he would always sidestep the issue by providing excuses and flattering the Queen. Apparently, Queen Elizabeth I was so put off by this that she is reported to have said, "This is all Blarney. What he says he rarely means."

When I return home, I'll be able to talk my way out of anything! It was a unique experience. We had to walk up 127 steps to the battlement, hold onto a guardrail, and lean way back to kiss the stone. It looks scary, but isn't actually dangerous at all. It used to be extremely difficult to access the Blarney Stone, so those who made the ascent and were able to kiss it were considered courageous and agile.

I will write to you again from our next stop—near the harbor town of Dun Laoghaire, where we will visit the James Joyce Tower.

Sláinte,
Michaela

Answer the questions about the e-mail

1. From where is Michaela writing? _____

2. Where is Cork located, and what did you learn about it?
_____
_____

3. What is the Blarney Stone?
_____
_____

4. Who built Blarney Castle and when was it erected?
_____

5. What is said to happen if you kiss the Blarney Stone?
_____

6. Do you think this is true? Explain.
_____

7. What is the origin of this story?
_____
_____

8. The Blarney Stone is one of Ireland's most popular destinations. Can you name three popular historic tourist destinations in the United States?
_____
_____

9. Where is Michaela's next stop?
_____

10. What do you think *sláinte* means? What language do you think it is?
_____

THE
BLARNEY
STONE

Literary Ireland

Ireland has a history steeped with extraordinary literary figures. Here are just two.

James Joyce

James Joyce was an Irish novelist and poet who lived between 1882 and 1941. Born in Dublin to a poor family, Joyce was raised in the Roman Catholic faith, but he broke his ties with the Church while in college. In 1904, Joyce left Dublin with a woman named Nora Barnacle, whom he eventually married. Over the course of their marriage, they lived in Trieste, Paris, and Zürich with their two children. Joyce was noted for his experimental use of language in such works as *Ulysses* and *Finnegans Wake*, making him one of the most influential writers of the 20th century. Joyce changed the face of the novel as a genre. He used complicated symbols drawn from mythology, history, and literature. He also utilized what could be called a unique language. He wove invented words, puns, and allusions through his writing. Joyce was also known for enhancing his work through an extensive use of interior monologue, which is a passage of a character's inner thoughts.

William Butler Yeats

William Butler Yeats was an Irish poet, dramatist, and Nobel laureate who is considered one of the foremost writers of the 20th century. He was born in 1865 in the seaside village of Sandymount, Ireland, and spent his childhood in Sligo. He lived the rest of his life between Sligo, Dublin, and London. Yeats took an interest in poetry as a child, and he was fascinated by Irish legends and the occult. Until about 1900, these topics were the focus of his work. But as he grew older, Yeats adopted many different ideological positions, and after the turn of the century, Yeats's poetry grew more physical and realistic. His work also explores the greater themes of life in contrast to art, and finding beauty in the mundane. The last years of his life produced his most intimate work. All the writing "periods" of Yeats's life have proved inspirational to writers worldwide. He died in 1939.

Compare and contrast the writers. Write a *J* if it applies to James Joyce, a *Y* if it applies to William Butler Yeats, a *B* if it applies to both writers, and an *N* if it applies to neither writer.

1. I was fascinated by Irish legends and the occult. _____

2. I was raised in the Roman Catholic faith, but I broke ties with the Church while in college. _____

3. I am often regarded as the chief representative of the Victorian age in poetry. _____

4. I wove invented words, puns, and allusions through my writing. _____

5. I was born in Ireland. _____

6. My work explored the greater themes of life in contrast to art. _____

7. I enhanced my work through an extensive use of interior monologue. _____

8. I was born in 1865 in the seaside village of Sandymount. _____

9. I was one of the most influential writers of the 20th century. _____

10. Based on prior knowledge of Irish history, why might Ireland have a history steeped with extraordinary literary figures? _____

_____

_____

_____

Yeats's Words

The Lake Isle of Innisfree
By William Butler Yeats 1892

1 I will arise and go now, and go to Innisfree,
2 And a small cabin build there, of clay and wattles made;
3 Nine bean rows will I have there, a hive for the honeybee,
4 And live alone in the bee-loud glade.

5 And I shall have some peace there, for peace comes dropping slow,
6 Dropping from the veils of the morning to where the cricket sings;
7 There midnight's all a-glimmer, and noon a purple glow,
8 And evening full of the linnet's wings.

9 I will arise and go now, for always night and day
10 I hear the water lapping with low sounds by the shore;
11 While I stand on the roadway, or on the pavements gray,
12 I hear it in the deep heart's core.

Answer the questions about the reading.

1. What genre of literature is this? _____

2. Who is the author? _____

3. When was it written? _____

4. What does the author explain in line 1?

_____

_____

5. What sort of place does he describe in lines 2 through 4?

_____

_____

_____

6. In line 5, what does the author tell you about how he feels about this place?

_____

7. What is nighttime like in this place? Underline the parts of lines 7 through 8 that tell you.

8. Lines 9 through 10 might be described as _____.

   tough   jerky   soothing

9. In line 11, where has the author taken us?

_____

10. To the author, does this place seem better or worse than the place described earlier? Explain.

_____

_____

_____

Defining Poetry

Poetry is a kind of writing in which the sound and meaning of groups of words express ideas or emotion in addition to the experiences or strong feelings the writer shares. Unlike most other forms of writing, poetry is often written in lines, rather than paragraphs. Poetry also sounds different from other forms of writing, often using rhythm and rhyme to create an interesting sound when read aloud. Poetry catches the attention of a reader because it appeals to both emotions and senses.

Sound is arguably the single most important aspect of any poem. The sound that any given word makes, or the sounds that come from specific groups of words used together, are what make poetry so unique as a form of writing. A typical story or report does not focus on the sounds that each individual word makes when read. But poems generally contain few words, so it is important that each word plays a role in making an impact on the reader. Rhythm is the flow of sounds created by successive words in a poem. When you read a poem you can often hear this repetitive pattern, or "beat," in the sounds. This is called meter.

Some of the oldest and best-known poetry in the world came from Ancient Greece. As far back as 700 BCE, poets there recited their work at public events and religious ceremonies. The great epic poems *The Iliad* and *The Odyssey* by Homer, pictured above, came from Greece. The Greeks eventually influenced Roman poets, such as Virgil, who wrote the *Aeneid* around 20 or 30 BCE. In medieval times, poems such as *Beowulf, The Divine Comedy* by Dante, and *The Canterbury Tales* by Chaucer were written. Religion and romance became the topic of choice for many poets at that time.

Poetry flourished even more during the Renaissance period of history, an era of many great cultural achievements. This was the period during which Shakespeare, the most well-known poet, was making his mark! Needless to say, a trend had started. Poetry has continued to grow and change as a form of literary expression in modern times.

Use the clues to find words from the reading in the word puzzle below.

1. most famous poet of all time

2. era of extraordinary music, art, and writing

3. poetry is often written in these, as opposed to paragraphs

4. most important aspect of any poem

5. flow of sounds created by words in a poem

6. a good poem can make a reader feel this

7. author of *The Iliad*

8. famous medieval poem

9. home of some of the oldest poetry

10. repetitive pattern in the sounds

D	M	E	R	E	N	A	I	S	S	A	N	C	E	I	L	E
R	O	E	H	D	I	S	S	O	C	T	E	G	O	F	D	S
O	E	N	Y	T	I	O	N	U	L	P	A	R	K	X	M	X
O	X	N	T	C	A	F	I	N	O	S	S	I	L	O	C	Z
S	F	L	H	R	I	D	A	D	A	B	T	H	E	L	L	J
E	I	M	M	O	R	T	A	L	E	E	M	O	T	I	O	N
V	N	L	T	G	O	L	S	T	F	O	U	K	I	N	O	I
M	E	T	E	R	N	O	A	G	H	W	M	E	S	E	R	L
L	T	A	M	E	C	H	U	Z	O	U	A	A	T	S	C	L
T	B	N	I	E	O	A	R	O	M	L	N	A	E	C	H	A
D	T	I	S	C	A	V	I	E	E	F	E	L	R	S	I	G
S	H	A	K	E	S	P	E	A	R	E	R	G	L	A	D	E

Poetry Forms

Common Forms of Poetry

Lyric: A short poem that expresses feelings.

Elegy: A sad poem usually written after a person's death.

Ode: A long, lyrical poem that uses a great deal of imagery.

Sonnet: A fourteen-line poem with a set rhyme scheme, which expresses feelings, most often love. Each line is ten syllables.

Haiku: A type of Japanese poem that is three lines long. The first line is five syllables, the second line is seven syllables, and the fifth line is five syllables.

Limerick: A funny, five-line poem with a set rhyme scheme. The first, second, and fifth lines rhyme with one another and each has three stressed syllables. The third and fourth lines rhyme with each other and each has two stressed syllables.

Narrative: A poem that tells a story.

Epic: A long poem that tells a story. The story is often about a hero on an adventure.

Ballad: A poem that tells a story that is often sad. Ballads are normally written in four-line stanzas in which the first and third lines have four accented syllables and the second and fourth lines have three accented syllables.

Blank Verse: A poem with regular rhythm but no rhyme.

Free Verse: poetry that does not require meter or rhyme.

Less Typical Forms of Poetry

Modern poets have adapted the classic forms of poetry in their own ways. They've spiced up old favorites, and the world of poetry is a more interesting place for it!

Alphabet poetry: A form in which a single letter in sections of the alphabet serve as the first letter in each line of the poem.

Name poetry: A form in which a single letter in a complete name serves as the first letter in each line of the poem.

Title-down poetry: A form in which the letters that spell the subject of the poem are used as the first letter of each line.

List poetry: A form that lists words or phrases.

Phrase poetry: a form in which an idea is stated by listing phrases.

Concrete poetry: A form in which the lines of the poem form a shape on the page. The shape helps express the meaning of the poem.

Definition poetry: A form in which a word or an idea is defined in a creative way.

Terse verse: A form in which two rhyming words with the same number of syllables make up each line.

Identify the form of each poem.

1. Daring to run
   Out of the house, he
   Goes dashing down the street!
   Poetry form: _____

2. Night; and once again,
   All the while I wait for you,
   cold wind turns into rain.
   Poetry form: _____

3. Loving is caring
   Loving is sharing
   Loving is growing
   Into who you are and loving that person.
   Poetry form: _____

4. Rats in the garbage bins
   Squirming all around.
   Trash makes them climb
   Under the lids to feast!
   Poetry form: _____

5. Fall
   Ball
   Poetry form: _____

6. There was an Old Man of Vienna,
   Who lived upon Tincture of Senna;
   When that did not agree,
   He took Chamomile Tea,
   That nasty Old Man of Vienna.
   Poetry form: _____

Your Poetry

Using any one of the styles of poetry mentioned on the previous pages, write your own poem. Make sure to adhere to the rules of the form you choose.

Poetry to a Beat

Listen carefully to the words of your favorite song, which is really just a poem set to music. Interpret its meaning in the same way you interpreted the Yeats poem on page 116.

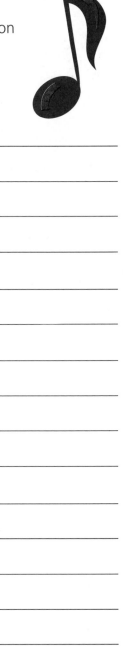

Frosty Evening

Stopping by Woods on a Snowy Evening
By Robert Frost

1 Whose woods these are I think I know.
2 His house is in the village though;
3 He will not see me stopping here
4 To watch his woods fill up with snow.

5 My little horse must think it queer
6 To stop without a farmhouse near
7 Between the woods and frozen lake
8 The darkest evening of the year.

9 He gives his harness bells a shake
10 To ask if there is some mistake.
11 The only other sound's the sweep
12 Of easy wind and downy flake.

13 The woods are lovely, dark and deep.
14 But I have promises to keep,
15 And miles to go before I sleep,
16 And miles to go before I sleep.

Answer the questions about the poem.

1. It is the middle of winter. *True* or *false*? _____

2. The speaker considers his horse's thoughts. *True* or *false*? _____

3. The speaker has lost his way. *True* or *false*? _____

4. The speaker admires the snowy woods and is attracted to its stark beauty and solitude. *True* or *false*? _____

5. The speaker feels the pull of responsibility. *True* or *false*? _____

6. The owner of the woods and the speaker do not get along. *True* or *false*?

_____

7. Who is the author of this poem?

_____

A stanza is the division in a poem, which are based on the number of lines it contains.

Couplet: a two-line stanza

Triplet: a three-line stanza

Quatrain: a four-line stanza

Cinquain: a five-line stanza

Sestet: a six-line stanza

Septet: a seven-line stanza

Octave: an eight-line stanza

8. How many stanzas are in this poem? _____

9. How many lines are there in each stanza? What is the term for this type of stanza?

_____

10. How many syllables are in each line of the poem? _____

The Atmosphere

Deep in space, temperatures can be –450° Fahrenheit—chilly, to say the least! But near the sun, temperatures reach thousands of degrees Fahrenheit. Where does earth fall among these temperature extremes? Earth's temperatures are very moderate in comparison, but why is that? The cause is simple: our atmosphere.

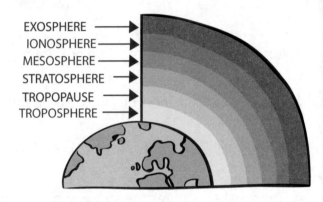

Earth's atmosphere separates our planet from the inhospitable climate of space. It is several hundred miles thick and is composed of different gases, primarily nitrogen and oxygen, but also carbon dioxide, ozone, and other gases. Earth's atmosphere serves as a cocoon, keeping our planet warm and protecting us from the direct effects of the sun's radiation. Without the atmosphere, earth could not sustain life.

The atmosphere is composed of several layers: troposphere, tropopause, stratosphere, mesosphere, ionosphere, and exosphere. The layer closest to earth is the troposphere. Most of the clouds in the sky are found in the troposphere, and so this layer of the atmosphere is associated with weather. The troposphere contains a variety of gases—water vapor, carbon dioxide, methane, nitrous oxide, and others—which help retain heat, a portion of which is then radiated back to warm the surface of earth. It extends up to ten miles above the earth's surface and its temperature generally decreases as altitude increases.

The transition layer between the troposphere and the stratosphere is called the tropopause. This part of the atmosphere is characterized by little or no change in temperature as altitude increases.

The next layer is called the stratosphere, which extends from about 6 to 30 miles above the surface of earth. The stratosphere is characterized by fewer clouds and a slight temperature increase with altitude. The stratosphere includes the ozone, whose molecules absorb ultraviolet radiation from the sun and protect us from its harmful effects. Its maintenance is crucial for our survival. In the lower stratosphere are the highest clouds, such as cirrus, cirrostratus, and cirrocumulus clouds.

The next layer of the atmosphere is the coldest. The mesosphere is between 30 to 50 miles above the surface of earth. Its temperatures decrease quickly as height increases.

Above the mesosphere is the ionosphere, which is also called the thermosphere. This layer extends about 50 to 400 miles from the surface of earth, and its temperatures can reach up to several thousand degrees Fahrenheit. The ionosphere contains its namesake ions, as well as free electrons. The ions are created when sunlight hits atoms and tears off some electrons. The phenomenon known as aurora, or the Northern Lights and Southern Lights, occurs in the ionosphere.

Finally, beyond the ionosphere is the exosphere. It is the outermost layer of the atmosphere and extends about 500 to 800 miles above the surface of earth. The exosphere is the transition zone into space, and its lower boundary is called the critical level of escape.

Answer the questions about the reading.

1. Which layer of earth's atmosphere is the coldest? _____
   mesosphere   troposphere   exosphere

2. The atmosphere is composed of what different gases? Write the letter of the answer. _____
   a. carbon dioxide   **b.** ozone   **c.** nitrogen and oxygen

3. This layer of the atmosphere is hot stuff. _____
   ionosphere   troposphere   mesosphere

4. This layer is home to cirrus, cirrostratus, and cirrocumulus clouds.
   _____

5. You are in Alaska and see bands of light dancing in the sky. Where are they coming from?
   _____

6. What gases are found in the troposphere? Underline them in the reading.

7. This layer of the atmosphere is known as a transition layer. _____

8. In which layer of the atmosphere is the ozone? _____

9. If the ozone were to be depleted, would we be in danger? Explain.

   _____

   _____

   _____

10. What have you heard is happening to the ozone? What are the causes of this?

   _____

   _____

   _____

   _____

Hole in the Sky

Earth's ozone has a very important task: protecting us from the sun. While we do need the sun's energy, its powerful ultraviolet rays would be harmful to earth if they hit our planet with their full impact. The crucial ozone filters the sun's radiation, making the layer's presence absolutely vital for our survival.

To understand the possible effects of losing the ozone, recall the last time you had sunburn. This burning of the skin is caused by ultraviolet (UV) light from the sun. The sun's radiation also causes cancer, weakens our immune systems, and has other harmful effects. Fortunately, the ozone absorbs almost all of the harmful UV radiation. Ozone forms when oxygen molecules (O_2) are split by ultraviolet radiation into two separate oxygen atoms (O), and these single oxygen atoms can collide with oxygen molecules. The result is O_3—ozone!

Ozone is a form of oxygen that unfortunately can be destroyed easily by certain manmade chemicals. You have likely heard that there is a "hole" in the ozone layer. Scientists believe that ozone is being destroyed as a result of pollution, specifically the use of chlorofluorocarbons (CFCs), which are manmade chemicals used for purposes such as refrigeration. When they floated up into the stratosphere, CFCs reacted with ultraviolet radiation to create chlorine. When chlorine reacted with ozone, the chemical damaged the layer. In 1987, the leading industrial countries agreed to stop using these chemicals, but their effects may continue to be felt for a number of years to come. CFCs linger in the troposphere for years before reaching the stratosphere and the ozone layer.

The "hole" in the ozone is most severe in the polar regions of the world. In fact, in 2006, scientists reported that the hole over Antarctica was the largest it's ever been—an average of 10.6 million square miles. That's larger than the surface area of North America!

But there is good news! Scientists project that within the next few decades, ozone depletion from CFCs will peak and then gradually dissipate. If CFCs had not been banned in the 1980s, the situation would be a lot worse. In fact, scientists predict that by the year 2070, the big ozone holes will be a thing of the past.

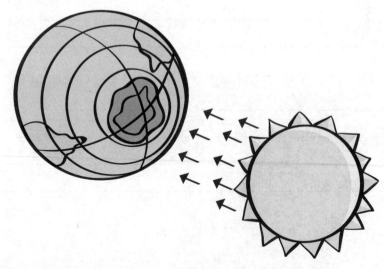

Answer the questions about the reading.

1. Which statement is correct? Write the letter of the answer. _____
   a. Humans will get better tans without the ozone in the way.
   b. The hole in the ozone is a result of human pollution.
   c. The hole in the ozone will be there forever.

2. In what layer of the atmosphere is the ozone? _____

3. What is the main purpose served by the ozone?
   _____

4. In what parts of the world is ozone depletion the most serious?
   _____

5. Based on prior knowledge, what natural light phenomenon can be seen there?
   _____

6. What important thing happened in 1987?
   _____
   _____

7. Why is ozone depletion still an issue today?
   _____
   _____

8. If CFCs had not been banned in the 1980s, then _____
   _____ .

Circle the cause-effect relationships below.

9. a. Sunburn is caused by the ozone.
   b. Sunburn is caused by sunblock.
   c. Sunburn is caused by ultraviolet (UV) light from the sun.

10. a. CFCs caused a hole to form in the ozone.
    b. Banning CFCs caused a hole in the ozone.
    c. Polar regions of the world have caused a hole to form in the ozone.

Water Pollution

When people envision water pollution, images of trash-filled rivers and oil-covered birds typically come to mind. But there is another type of water pollution that exists, and the water is actually the source of it!

Millions of people worldwide have come to believe that drinking bottled water is safer and better for their health. Bottled water is indeed a fast and convenient way to have water available, but it comes at a price: all those plastic bottles use a lot of fossil fuels and pollute the environment.

This is a problem in the United States more than anywhere else because of the rates of consumption here: Americans buy more bottled water than any other nation in the world, adding 29 billion water bottles a year to the problem. In order to make all these bottles, manufacturers use 17 million barrels of crude oil. That's enough oil to keep a million cars operating for an entire year! The water itself often comes from faraway places such as France, Iceland, or Maine, which means it has to travel to your local store somehow. Unlike tap water, which relies on a mostly preexisting infrastructure of underground pipes and plumbing, bottled water delivery burns fossil fuels and results in the release of thousands of tons of harmful emissions. Since some bottled water is also shipped or stored cold, electricity is expended for refrigeration. There is also growing concern that chemicals in plastic bottles may leach into the water, making bottled water dangerous.

Americans have stopped relying on the tap as a water source because of the belief that bottled water is cleaner. In the United States, local governments make sure water from the faucet is safe. While old pipes and outdated treatment can indeed threaten tap water quality, this problem can be easily resolved with at-home filtration devices.

In order to reduce the amount of pollution cause by plastic water bottles, turn on the faucet instead! You can also recycle, though few Americans do so. Unfortunately, for every six water bottles we use, only one makes it to the recycling bin. The rest are sent to landfills, or end up as trash on the land and in rivers, lakes, and the ocean. Plastic bottles require many hundreds of years to disintegrate. Instead of going out with the trash, plastic bottles can be turned into items like carpeting or fleece clothing. And recycling just one bottle can save enough energy to power a 60-watt light bulb for six hours.

Answer the questions about the reading.

1. What is the ultimate goal of this reading? Circle all that apply.

inform   persuade   entertain

2. How does the title make you consider what this reading is about?

_____

_____

3. Where does a lot of bottled water come from?

_____

4. What are the effects of this?

_____

_____

5. Can the water inside a bottle be dangerous at all? Explain.

_____

_____

6. Who drinks more bottled water than anyone else? _____

7. How can recycling plastic water bottles benefit earth?

_____

_____

8. What can be made from recycled plastic?

_____

9. What concession does the author make in this reading? Does that seem counterintuitive to you?

_____

_____

10. What is its effect? Explain.

_____

_____

_____

Harry Potter

Harry Potter is the namesake of a series of fantasy novels written for young readers by British author J. K. Rowling. The Harry Potter series chronicles the life of a young wizard, Harry, and his adventures at Hogwarts School of Witchcraft and Wizardry. Throughout the series, Harry struggles against the evil wizard Lord Voldemort. Since the release of the first book in 1998, the Harry Potter series has become nothing short of a phenomenon.

J. K. Rowling planned the series as a seven-book sequence, with each book bringing the reader through one year of Harry's secondary school career at Hogwarts. In the books, Rowling delves into two central ideas: Harry as a schoolboy and Harry as a wizard. What makes these books stand apart from others that explore similar topics is the fact that Rowling does not avoid the serious or frightening. The Harry Potter series depicts everything from self-sacrifice to death, which has enabled the books to successfully cross the boundary between adults' and children's books.

The Harry Potter books have garnered an enormous fan base. They have sold hundreds of millions of copies and have been translated into more than 64 languages. The immense popularity of the novels has spawned a media and entertainment empire, including feature films, video games, and many other types of Potter-themed merchandise.

Book	Year Published (in the U.S.)
1. *Harry Potter and the Sorcerer's Stone*	1998
2. *Harry Potter and the Chamber of Secrets*	1999
3. *Harry Potter and the Prisoner of Azkaban*	1999
4. *Harry Potter and the Goblet of Fire*	2000
5. *Harry Potter and the Order of the Phoenix*	2003
6. *Harry Potter and the Half-Blood Prince*	2005
7. *Harry Potter and the Deathly Hallows*	2007

Answer the questions about the reading.

1. Who is the protagonist of the Harry Potter books? _____

2. Who is the antagonist of the books? _____

3. Who is the author of the Harry Potter books? _____

4. What two main aspects of the main character does the author explore in these books?
_____

5. Match each book to its year of publication in the United States.

Harry Potter and the Sorcerer's Stone	2000
Harry Potter and the Chamber of Secrets	1999
Harry Potter and the Half-Blood Prince	2007
Harry Potter and the Goblet of Fire	1998
Harry Potter and the Order of the Phoenix	2005
Harry Potter and the Prisoner of Azkaban	2003
Harry Potter and the Deathly Hallows	1999

6. What makes these books stand out from others like them?
_____
_____

7. Have you ever read any of the Harry Potter books? Which ones?
_____
_____

8. If so, what did you think of them?
_____
_____

9. Have you ever heard any negative criticism of the books? Explain.
_____
_____

10. If the author were to write one more volume for the series, what do you think might happen in it?
_____
_____

Diagon Alley

In Harry Potter's world, magic hides in ordinary places. If you were to tap just the right brick in the wall behind the Leaky Cauldron in London, you would reveal a hallway that leads to Diagon Alley, a street containing an assortment of shops and restaurants. Diagon Alley serves as the hub of commerce in the wizarding world. Here are some of the wizarding businesses stationed there:

Madam Malkin's Robes for All Occasions
Gringotts Wizarding Bark
Stationery Shop
Quality Quidditch Supplies
Junk Shop
Second-Hand Robe Shop
Cauldron Shop
Apothecary
Magical Menagerie
Eeylops Owl Emporium
Magical Instruments
Florean Fortescue's Ice Cream Parlor

In addition, branching off Diagon Alley is Knockturn Alley, where wizards can purchase giant spiders, shrunken heads, and poisonous candles.

Answer the questions about Diagon Alley.

1. What is Diagon Alley?

_____

_____

2. Where is Diagon Alley?

_____

3. How does one enter Diagon Alley?

_____

4. On what other alley can wizards purchase supplies?

_____

5. How many stores could you visit to purchase a robe? _____

6. Where might one go to buy a huge, metal pot?

_____

7. Where might one go to purchase a broomstick for Quidditch?

_____

8. Where might one go to purchase a white rabbit?

_____

9. Where might a student purchase an owl?

_____

10. Where might one go for a cold treat?

_____

Rowling's World

J. K. (Joanne Kathleen) Rowling is the author of the enormously popular series of children's books about a boy named Harry Potter. The success of the novels has made Rowling the highest-earning novelist in history and the wealthiest woman in Great Britain. But life wasn't always so blessed for this talented writer.

Rowling was born in Yate, a small town in southern England. From the age of six, when she wrote her very first story, Rowling knew that she would be a writer. She grew up in Chepstow, England, and then attended Exeter University, where she earned a French and classics degree. After graduating from Exeter, she worked in various jobs while writing fiction for adults.

At age 26, Rowling moved to Portugal, where she taught English and later married a Portuguese journalist. During this time in her life she began writing a book about an orphaned boy who lives with his mean-spirited aunt and uncle, and who does not know that he is actually a wizard with magic powers. During the next five years, Rowling outlined the plots for each of seven books in a series and began writing the first novel.

By 1995, Rowling was divorced, and she moved to Edinburgh, Scotland. She was no longer able to afford childcare, so she went on public assistance. But Rowling persisted in her endeavor. She continued writing her book, often jotting down passages in cafés while her daughter slept at her side.

Rowling's finished manuscript was rejected by a number of publishers. But in 1996 she received an offer of publication, and in 1998, the world was introduced to Harry Potter. The rest, as they say, is (literary) history.

Answer the questions about the reading.

1. What is J. K. Rowling's full name?

_____

2. Why do you think she might have used her initials as her name on her novels?

_____

3. At one point in her life, J. K. Rowling was on public assistance. This is equivalent to

_____.

wealth   middle-class lifestyle   welfare

4. How do you think she must have felt at that point in her life?

_____

5. How do you think she must feel about her current success?

_____

6. Number the events of her life in the correct order.

_____ Rowling moved to Portugal, where she taught English.

_____ She grew up in Chepstow, England.

_____ Rowling was divorced, and she moved to Edinburgh, Scotland.

_____ Her first Harry Potter book was published.

_____ She earned a French and classics degree.

7. What happened the first several times Rowling tried to have her book published?

_____

8. How would this make you feel, if you were her?

_____

_____

Ton-Tongue Toffees

According to *Harry Potter and the Goblet of Fire*, these sweet treats are imbued with a wizard's engorgement charm that makes a person's tongue swell up to ten times its normal size. But they sure are delicious!

Ingredients:

2 cups sugar

8 tablespoons butter

$\frac{1}{2}$ teaspoon vanilla extract

$1\frac{1}{2}$ cups water

Directions:

1. Have an adult help you mix all ingredients in a medium saucepan and melt over medium heat until sugar is completely dissolved.
2. Boil until mixture reaches 290°F (use a candy thermometer).
3. Pour mixture into a greased or buttered 9 x 12" pan and let cool until almost firm to the touch.
4. With a sharp knife, score surface into two-inch squares, but do not cut completely.
5. When cool, break into pieces (this should be easy if toffee was properly scored).
6. Enjoy! Makes $1\frac{1}{4}$ pounds of toffee.

Answer the questions about the recipe.

1. Number the recipe steps in the correct order.

_____ Pour mixture into a greased or buttered 9 x 12" pan.

_____ With a sharp knife, score surface into two-inch squares.

_____ Boil until mixture reaches 290°F.

_____ When cool, break into pieces.

_____ Have an adult help you mix all ingredients in a medium saucepan.

2. What does the word *imbued* mean?

_____

3. What special thing do wizards add to this candy?

_____

4. What effect does it have on the person who eats it?

_____

_____

5. What do you think might happen if you do not score the candy well?

_____

6. How much toffee does this recipe yield? _____

7. How should you measure the temperature of the cooking candy? Write the letter of the answer.

_____

a. by sticking your finger in

b. by using a candy thermometer

c. by using a meat thermometer

8. What size pan is required for this recipe? _____

9. What do you think might happen if you did not butter the pan?

_____

_____

10. Circle all the ingredients that are **not** called for in the recipe.

butter	sugar	milk	eggs	water
nuts	vanilla extract	baking powder	brown sugar	

Branches of Magic at Hogwarts

Below are some popular types of magic taught at Hogwarts School of Wizardry and Witchcraft in the Harry Potter series.

Arithmancy: Abranch of magic concerned with the magical properties of numbers.

Herbology: The study of magical plants and fungi, including their care and their magical properties and uses. Some magical plants form important ingredients in potions, while others have magical effects on their own.

Legilimency: A branch of magic that extracts emotions and memories from another person's mind.

Occlumency: The art of magically defending the mind against external penetration so that it cannot be intruded upon and influenced. It is the defensive counter to Legilimency.

Transfiguration: Magic that changes one object into another. The opposite of Transfiguration is Untransfiguration, which is the process of returning something to its proper form.

Charms: A type of magic spell concerned with enchanting an object to behave in a way that isn't normal for that object. *Charm* tends to be a catchall term for any spell that isn't a Transfiguration. A well-chosen Charm is a powerful magical tool against a curse, jinx, and or hex.

Dark Arts: A negative form of magic. Typical Dark Magic spells are curses, hexes, or jinxes. Dark Magic could involve tampering with the free will of another person, or even killing another person.

Divination: Magic that attempts to foresee future events. Methods include crystal balls, visions, tarot cards, and smoke patterns.

Identify the type of magic used to create each effect described below.

1. changing a person's ears from human into rabbit ears   _____

2. discovering the magical properties of the number seven   _____

3. making a prophecy about future events   _____

4. using a Killing Curse   _____

5. working with dangerous plants, such as Devil's Snare   _____

6. causing an object to levitate   _____

7. pulling a memory of a parent's death from someone's mind   _____

8. defeating a Legilimen's lie-detector abilities   _____

9. a type of magic that is not a Transfiguration   _____

10. the defensive counter to Legilimency   _____

More Magic

Invent another branch of magic that could be practiced in Harry Potter's world and describe it here. Include detailed explanations of what is involved, what the possible effects are, and even how it might be misused.

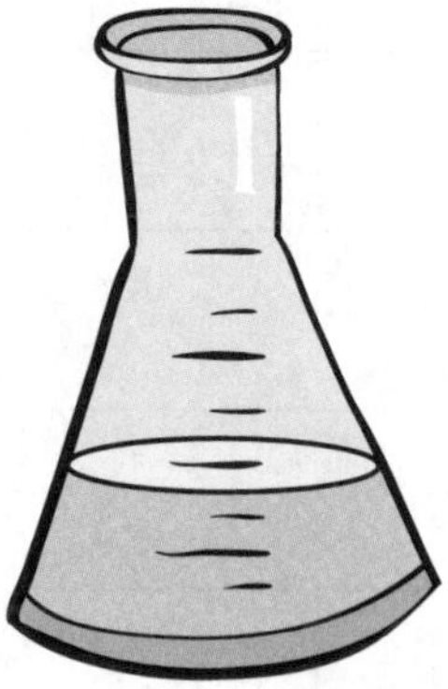

_____

_____

_____

_____

_____

_____

_____

_____

_____

_____

_____

_____

_____

_____

_____

_____

Your Magic

Spells play an important role in Hogwarts School. Try making up several of your own spells. Use the following as an example:

Duro (DUR-oh)

"duro" : to harden, solidify.

Turns a target object to stone.

_____

_____

_____

_____

_____

_____

_____

_____

_____

How to Play Quidditch

Quidditch is a magical game played by Harry Potter and his friends. Read all about it below.

You'll Need:
2 teams of seven players each
1 Quaffel
2 Bluggers
2 Blugger bats
1 Golden Snitch
Brooms for each player to fly on
6 Goal hoops (three at each of the opposite sides of the field)

How to Play

Step 1: Pick three players to be Chasers. These players need to fly around the field while passing the Quaffel back and forth. Chasers try to score goals by throwing the Quaffel through one of the opposite team's three hoops.

Step 2: Choose one player as a Goalie. The Goalie's job is to protect the three hoops so that the other team cannot score.

Step 3: Find two players to be Beaters. Beaters fly around the field and use small bats to hit Bluggers at the other team's players. Beaters protect their teammates by ensuring that the Bluggers are always heading toward the other team.

Step 4: Pick one player as the Seeker. The Seeker scans the field for the Golden Snitch, a small ball with wings. When the Seeker sees the snitch, he flies after it. It is the Seeker's job to catch it before the other team's Seeker.

Scoring

Step 1: Gain points by throwing the Quaffel through the other team's hoops. Each time the Quaffel passes through the hoops, the scoring team receives 10 points.

Step 2: Gain 150 points when the seeker catches the Golden Snitch.

Step 3: Win Quidditch by catching the Golden Snitch. Once a Seeker catches the Golden Snitch, the game is over.

Answer the questions about the game.

1. Who is the most important player in Quidditch? _____

2. What do players travel on when playing Quidditch? _____

3. How is Quidditch won?

_____

4. How does one score points?

_____

_____

_____

5. How many goal hoops are there? _____

6. What is a Goalie's job?

_____

_____

7. How many points are awarded when the Seeker catches the Golden Snitch? _____

8. What do Beaters do?

_____

_____

9. If you were a Quidditch player, what position would you be? Explain.

_____

_____

10. Do you think Quidditch sounds like a difficult game to master? Explain.

_____

_____

_____

Get Some Zs

Most adolescents need about nine hours of sleep each night. The proper amount of sleep is essential for anyone to be fully functional and alert. Being sleep deprived has numerous negative effects, so receiving enough Zs is vital.

Research shows that lost sleep can lead to poorer grades and hinder athletic ability. Lack of sleep has also been linked to emotional issues, such as depression. Sleep also helps keep us physically healthy by slowing our body's systems enough to restore us after a long day of being active.

The fact that adolescents require more sleep than adults—who on average need about eight hours of sleep—is not because of laziness, but rather, because of their biological clocks. An adolescent's circadian rhythm is temporarily reset during this portion of life, telling the body to fall asleep later and wake up later. This change in the circadian rhythm seems to be due to the brain hormone melatonin's production later at night for adolescents than for kids and adults. This lack of melatonin early at night makes falling asleep early more difficult for adolescents.

Unfortunately, this change in circadian rhythm happens at a time in a person's life when he or she happens to be getting busier and busier. School is more demanding, and many things draw on the time of an adolescent, such as sports, clubs, and socializing. School also may start earlier as adolescents enter middle school and then high school. The ultimate effect is that they aren't able to fall asleep until late, but still have to get up very early for a busy day. This can lead to severe sleep deprivation.

Answer the questions about the reading.

1. Place a check next to the the main idea of the reading.

____ An adolescent's circadian rhythm is temporarily reset during this portion of life.

____ Sleep deprivation has numerous negative effects, so receiving enough Zs is vital for young people.

____ Lack of sleep has been linked to emotional issues, such as depression.

2. What do you think the phrase *circadian rhythm* in paragraph 3 means? Write the letter of the answer. ____

a. chirping of crickets   **b.** flow of music   **c.** 24-hour biological clock

3. What does the word *deprived* in paragraph 1 mean?

_____

4. How much more sleep do adolescents need than adults, on average?

_____

5. Research shows that lost sleep can lead to poorer grades and hinder athletic ability. *True* or *false*?

_____

6. Adolescents require more sleep than adults because they are lazy. *True* or *false*?

_____

7. Lack of sleep has been linked to emotional issues, such as depression. *True* or *false*?

_____

8. What does the word *hinder* in paragraph 2 mean?

_____

9. Based on the information provided, what do you think melatonin does?

_____

10. How does not sleeping enough make you feel? Do you agree with the author's viewpoint, based on your own experiences?

_____

_____

_____

Good Sleep Hygiene

Sleep specialists all agree that practicing good sleep hygiene, or healthy regimen, is the best way to give your body the rest it needs.

Set a regular bedtime.
Going to bed and waking up at the same time each day establishes sleep patterns. Try to stick to your sleep schedule, even on weekends.

Avoid caffeine.
After about 4 PM, do not ingest caffeine or any other stimulating foods or drinks. Caffeine keeps you awake and its effects can last for hours.

Don't nap too much.
If you are napping for longer than 30 minutes during the day, this extra sleep may keep you from falling asleep later.

Exercise regularly.
Challenging your body daily, especially in the late afternoon, can help a person sleep. But try not to exercise right before bed, as it can arouse your system too much, making sleep harder to come by.

Relax your mind.
Before bedtime, avoid watching television, especially violent, scary, or action-packed movies or programs. The light from the screen and the plot can set your mind and heart racing.

Unwind by keeping the lights low.
Dim lighting tells your body that it's time to be calm and relaxed. Toward the end of the day, turn off bright overhead lights to help your body begin to feel sleepy.

Create the proper sleeping environment.
People sleep best in a quiet, dark, cool room. Close your blinds or curtains and turn down the thermostat in your room.

Wake up with bright light.
Bright light in the morning signals to your body that it's time to get going. So, throw your shades open when you wake, or invest in an alarm clock that wakes you with light.

Answer the questions about the reading.

1. Unscramble the words mentioned in the reading.

minrnog _____

peelsing nevrionnmet _____

epels neegihy _____

fneiefac _____

recixcese _____

2. What would happen if you went to sleep and woke up at the same time every school day, but then on weekends, slept until noon and stayed up very late?

_____

_____

3. Predict how you would feel at night if you exercised every afternoon.

_____

4. Predict how you would feel at night if you exercised every night before bedtime.

_____

5. Predict how you would feel if you never exercised at all.

_____

_____

6. What would happen if you drank a caffeinated energy drink and watched a horror movie before bed?

_____

_____

School Hours

Recently, some people have suggested that middle school classes begin later in the morning to accommodate adolescents' need for more sleep. Some schools have already implemented later start times. Do you feel that this is a good idea? Write a letter to the school district in which you lobby for or against this idea. Be certain to use proper business letter format, clearly state your opinion, provide supporting reasons, and offer a course of action.

Dream Journal

Recording your dreams is a useful way to help remember them. By writing down your dreams immediately upon waking, you are able to preserve details, many of which are otherwise rapidly forgotten, no matter how memorable the dream originally seemed.

In the space provided, start your own dream journal. Record every dream you have for the next few nights by either writing them down or drawing them here.

El Niño

You have likely heard about El Niño recently, either on the news or in everyday conversation. This mysterious force is often blamed for wreaking havoc with the weather. In short, El Niño is a climate pattern that causes irregular warming in the ocean surface temperatures from the coasts of Peru and Ecuador to the equatorial central Pacific. While this pattern can be unpredictable, scientists continue to study it, as it has important consequences for weather around the globe.

The El Niño phenomenon usually occurs once every 4 years and lasts for about 18 months at a time. South American fishermen gave it the name *El Niño*, a Spanish term for "The Little Boy," because they noticed it often happened around Christmastime, when, according to Christian belief, Jesus Christ was born.

El Niño is one part of the Southern Oscillation, a seesaw pattern of surface air pressure levels fluctuating between the eastern and western tropical Pacific. Scientists do not really understand how El Niño forms, but its effects have become quite evident.

Usually, El Niño brings rain and warmer temperatures. Warm water along the equator displaces, or takes the place of, colder water found in the Humbolt Current, which is farther north. This displacement has caused the sea temperatures off the coast of South America to become three to five degrees higher than usual. From 1982 to 1983, El Niño brought flooding to California, Utah, and Louisiana. It is believed that El Niño may have contributed to both the 1993 Mississippi and 1995 California floods, as well as drought conditions in South America, Africa, and Australia.

Unfortunately, not all El Niños behave in the same way, nor does the atmosphere always react in the same way from one El Niño to another. So scientists at NASA continue to study El Niño events. They cannot change the fact that El Niños occur, but they can attempt to provide sufficient warning so that populations can be better prepared to deal with the repercussions of El Niño.

Answer the questions about the reading.

1. Have you ever heard of El Niño? What did you think it was?

_____

_____

2. What causes El Niño?

_____

3. Do you feel that scientists should continue to learn more about El Niño? Why?

_____

_____

4. What does the term *El Niño* mean? Underline the part that tells you.

5. When does El Niño occur and for how long?

_____

_____

6. Circle the term below that best describes El Niño.

normal   volatile   foreseeable

7. What are *repercussions*? Write the letter of the answer. _____

   a. reciprocal reasons   **b.** reciprocal causes   **c.** reciprocal effects

8. Can scientists stop El Niño?

_____

9. What are two negative effects of El Niño?

_____

10. Can you think of another natural phenomenon that has been changing the state of the oceans?

_____

Devil Toad

Scientists recently made a remarkable discovery: a bowling ball–sized frog lived among dinosaurs millions of years ago! This prehistoric creature had heavy armor on its body, had teeth, and was about 16 inches long and weighed 10 pounds. That's one enormous frog! The creature's stature and appearance was so intimidating that scientists dubbed the beast *Beelzebufo*, or Devil Toad, coming from *Beelzebub*, the Greek word for "devil," and *bufo*, Latin for "toad."

Paleontologist David Krause of Stony Brook University led the team working to determine the Devil Toad's origins and history. In 1993, Krause began uncovering fragments of abnormally large frog bones on the island of Madagascar, off the eastern coast of Africa. After studying the bones, the team determined that they dated back to the late Cretaceous period, roughly 70 million years ago. But many years passed before Krause and his team of experts could assemble enough bones to "piece together" the creature.

Strangely, the Devil Toad does not seem to be a relative of the largest living frog, the Goliath frog of West Africa, which can reach seven pounds. Rather, the Devil Toad was probably a relative of South American horned frogs, known scientifically as Ceratophrys. Like its modern cousins, the Devil Toad had a wide mouth, powerful jaws, and teeth. Its skull bones were particularly thick, with ridges and grooves characteristic of some type of armor, or protective covering. Krause indicated that the Devil Toad might have been voracious enough to finish off baby dinosaurs!

While the bones were found near Africa, the Devil Toad's South American ancestry challenges assumptions about ancient geography. The theory of continental drift says that what is now Madagascar would have been long separated from South America by ocean during the Devil Toad's existence. In addition, frogs can't survive long in a saltwater environment, so having swam between the two landmasses is unlikely. Krause believes that the Devil Toad provides evidence for competing theories that a land bridge still connected Africa and South America that late in time.

Use the clues to find and circle words in the word puzzle below.

1. another name for Devil Toad

2. Devil Toad's continental home

3. scientist who studies fossils

4. scientific name for modern relative of Devil Toad

5. largest living frog

6. period in which Devil Toad lived

7. creature of which the Devil Toad may have been an enemy

8. protective covering

P	T	E	N	A	I	S	W	A	N	C	E	W	R	A
A	F	R	I	C	A	O	C	T	E	G	O	T	H	E
L	Y	T	I	O	N	U	L	P	A	D	K	Y	V	X
E	T	C	A	F	I	N	G	O	L	I	A	T	H	T
O	H	E	I	D	A	C	A	B	T	N	E	E	J	E
N	M	R	R	T	A	R	E	E	M	O	T	R	C	W
T	T	A	O	L	S	E	F	O	U	S	I	T	A	C
O	E	T	N	O	A	T	H	W	M	A	S	X	Y	A
L	M	O	C	H	U	A	O	U	A	U	T	H	H	R
O	I	P	O	A	R	C	M	L	N	R	E	E	B	M
G	S	H	A	B	E	E	L	E	Z	E	B	U	F	O
I	K	R	S	P	E	O	R	E	R	G	L	J	B	R
S	E	Y	A	T	H	U	V	R	W	S	A	C	X	G
T	R	S	J	W	Y	S	E	B	V	T	H	J	Y	R

System of Classification

To organize all of earth's millions of plants and animals, scientists have developed a hierarchical system of classification. This system is based on overall similarity among organisms and was introduced by the 18th-century Swedish botanist Carolus Linnaeus.

Linnaeus's system of classification separates animals and plants into kingdoms. These kingdoms are broken down into successively smaller, less inclusive groups, including phylums, subphylums, classes, orders, families, genera, and species. The class Mammalia, for example, is one of nine classes in the kingdom Animalia, phylum Chordata, subphylum Vertebrata.

Linnaeus used binomial nomenclature to create his system, in which each species of animal or plant receives a name consisting of two terms. The first term identifies the genus to which it belongs and the second term identifies the species itself. For example, the domestic cat is called *Felis domesticus*.

Linnaeus used Latin to name everything because scientists worldwide used the language and he wished to avoid potential confusion from incorporating many different languages. Scientists who study classification, called taxonomists or systemists, continue to classify life in a way that reflects proper evolutionary history. As they acquire new information, such as from newly discovered fossils or molecular genetics, they rearrange the current classification scheme, adding new species and moving species from one genus to another.

Here is an example of a classification:

Class Mammalia

    Order Rodentia

        Family Aplodontidae: Mountain Beaver

        Family Sciuidae: Squirrels

        Family Castoridae: Beavers

        Family Geomyidae: Pocket Gophers

        Family Heteromyidae: Pocket Mice and Kangaroo Rats

        Family Dipodidae: Jumping Mice

        Family Muridae: Mice and Rats

            Subfamily Arvicolinae: Voles and Relatives

            Subfamily Sigmodontinae: New World Sigmodontine Mice and Rats

        Family Erethizontidae: Porcupines

        Family Myocastoridae: Nutria

Answer the questions about the reading.

1. What does the word *hierarchical* in paragraph 1 mean?

_____

2. Who invented the system of classification used today?

_____

3. What do you think a botanist is?

_____

_____

4. In what language is the system of classification? _____

5. What is a taxonomist? _____

6. What possible effect could the discovery of the Devil Toad have on this system?

_____

_____

7. What does the word *successively* in paragraph 2 mean?

_____

8. In the given example of classification, what is the class? _____

9. In that same example, what is the order? _____

10. What would the kingdom, phylum, and subphylum be in this example?

_____

_____

Inside a Medieval Castle

A castle is a type of fortified dwelling that is characteristic of the Middle Ages. Feudal lords developed these private fortress-residences, which served to protect the people inside, since war was endemic to Medieval times. Below is a cross-section of a typical castle.

Moat: An important part of medieval defense at castles, the moat was a massive ditch surrounding a castle that was often filled with water to enhance the castle's security. The deep water was much more difficult for invaders to travel through rather than simply over land.

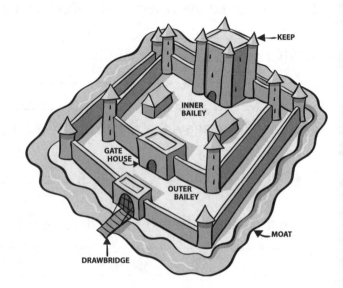

Outer bailey: The outer bailey was the first courtyard between the outer and inner walls of a castle. Enemies who had breached the outer walls could be stopped in the outer bailey and defenders could fire upon them from above.

Inner bailey: The inner courtyard of a castle.

Gatehouse: The gatehouse was the living quarters of the guards, located over the main gate of the castle. Over time, the gatehouse became heavily fortified and very important. Sometimes the owner of the castle chose to live in the gatehouse. Access to the palace grounds on this side could be made only through the drawbridge and gatehouse.

Drawbridge: The main entry to a castle, usually located over a moat. The drawbridge was perhaps one of the most important defensive features of a castle. The drawbridge could be raised or lowered. When raised, attackers were unable to enter the castle.

Keep: The keep contained the living quarters of the lord and his family, the rooms of state, and the prison cells. Because the castle was planned for security, the living quarters were rude, poorly lighted, and without provisions for comfort.

Use the reading and diagram to answer the questions.

1. Who developed castles and why?

_____

_____

2. What does the word *endemic* in paragraph 1 mean? Write the letter of the answer. ____
   a. characteristic of or prevalent in   **b.** obvious   **c.** hidden from invaders

3. What is a moat and what purpose did it serve?

_____

_____

4. What does the word *fortified* in paragraph 1 mean? Write the letter of the answer. ____
   a. made weak   **b.** made discreet   **c.** made strong

5. An enemy breaches the outer wall of the castle. What might happen?

_____

_____

6. What was the keep?

_____

_____

7. What was the most important defensive feature of a castle? Explain.

_____

_____

8. Were the castle's inhabitants comfortable? Explain.

_____

_____

9. If you were a feudal lord, would you have wanted to live in a castle? Why or why not?

_____

_____

10. If you lived in this castle, what forms of defense would you add or change? Write about them
   here.

_____

_____

_____

_____

Medieval Times

The Middle Ages was a period of history that extended from approximately the 5th century to the 15th century in Western Europe. On film, the Middle Ages, or Medieval times, is portrayed gloriously, with knights, castles, kings, banquets, and minstrels. While all of these things did exist, life during this time was actually dangerous and harsh.

Merely protecting oneself from physical harm was a major daily struggle at this point in history. For safety and defense, people formed small communities based around a lord or master in an arrangement called a feudal system. As part of the feudal system, the king awarded land grants called fiefs to the most important nobles and religious figures. In return, the king was given soldiers for his armies. The lord's manor consisted of a castle, a church, a village, and the surrounding farmland.

Peasants called serfs worked the land and produced the goods that the lord and manor needed. In exchange for living and working on his land, the lord offered these servants, who were nearly slaves, protection from harm, but this exchange carried significant hardship for serfs. They were heavily taxed and required to relinquish much of what they harvested from the farmland. The lord had the right to grant marriages and held absolute power to declare punishments for various offenses such as thievery or murder. The people were bound to their land plots, and when the land was sold, they were sold along with it. If the land they lived on changed ownership, they came under a new lord's jurisdiction.

In the 13th century, the feudal system began to decline, gradually giving way to the class system as the dominant form of social ranking.

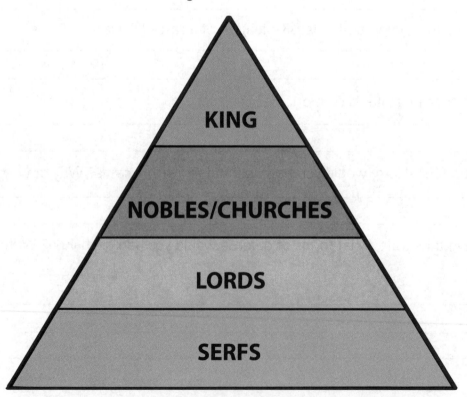

Answer the questions about the reading and the hierarchy chart.

1. Who is at the top of the hierarchy chart?

_____

2. Who is at the bottom of the hierarchy chart?

_____

3. Who do you think benefited the most from the feudal system? Explain.

_____

_____

4. When were the Middle Ages?

_____

5. Would you have liked being a serf? What were the benefits and drawbacks of being a serf?

_____

_____

6. What happened to a serf if the land on which he lived was sold?

_____

7. According to the reading, what was afforded to serfs for their efforts?

_____

8. What is a fief?

_____

9. Based on this reading, what do you think the ultimate goal of the feudal system was?

_____

_____

10. What does the word *thievery* in paragraph 3 mean?

_____

Medical Times

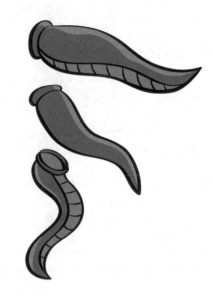

In the Middle Ages, medicine was much more loosely organized than it is today. At the time, medical treatment was considered a luxury, available mainly to the wealthy. Those living in villages rarely had the help of doctors, who practiced mostly in the cities and courts. A variety of medical practices were relied upon, including prayer, spells, and folk medicine.

Medical practice was often connected to the natural world. The underlying principle of medieval medicine was the theory of humors. It was believed that within every individual there were four principal fluids, called humors. They were black bile, yellow bile, phlegm, and blood. The four humors were also associated with the four seasons: black bile was connected to autumn, yellow bile to summer, phlegm to winter, and blood to spring.

The humors needed to be balanced for a person to remain healthy. For example, too much phlegm in the body caused lung problems, and the body tried to cough up the phlegm to restore a balance. The balance of humors in humans could be achieved by diet, medicines, and surgery.

Medical treatment during the Middle Ages was risky business. True doctors—that is, medically trained and licensed professionals as we have today—were few and far between. Often, people instead entrusted their health to healers, who relied on herbs and folk remedies, or saints, who relied on healing by miracle.

While surgery was considered a last resort, it was still a dicey endeavor. The most common form of surgery was bloodletting, in which a considerable amount of blood was drawn from a person's body in the hope that doing so would restore the balance of fluids in the body. Leeches, pictured above, were sometimes used to suck the blood out! Bloodletting was used to treat a wide range of diseases. For more severe surgeries, a patient would sometimes be given potions to relieve pain or induce sleep, much like anesthesia today. The problem was that sometimes the patient died as a result of the potions. Certain combinations of herbs and medicines proved lethal.

A great crisis in medicine occurred during the Middle Ages. In the 14th century, a plague called the Black Death became an epidemic. Because the prevailing medical theories focused on nature and religion rather than scientific explanations, Europeans did not fare well. The Black Death wiped out close to two-thirds of the population.

Answer the questions about the reading.

1. While surgery was considered a last resort, it was still a dicey endeavor. *Fact* or *opinion*?

_____

2. Medical practice was often connected to the natural world. *Fact* or *opinion*?

_____

3. A variety of medical practices were relied upon, including prayer, spells, and folk medicine. *Fact* or *opinion*? _____

4. Bloodletting was a great way to treat a wide range of diseases. *Fact* or *opinion*?

_____

5. The Black Death wiped out close to two-thirds of the population of Europe. *Fact* or *opinion*? _____

6. What is an antonym for *luxury* in paragraph 1? Circle all that apply.
treat   base   indulgence   fundament   necessity
requirement   extravagance

7. What is an epidemic? Can you think of any others that have occurred?

_____

_____

8. One bloodletting tool was a _____.

9. How would you feel if a doctor told you that he wanted to drain a lot of your blood? How would you feel if he used the tool mentioned above to do so?

_____

_____

10. What were humors? _____

11. What was the significance of humors?

_____

_____

Black Death

Starting around 1348, the bubonic plague ravaged the continents of Europe and Asia, killing an estimated forty million people. This epidemic has come to be known as the Black Death. Its victims suffered a horribly painful death characterized by fever and dying, blackened flesh.

Although they are not certain, many historians agree that the Black Death probably originated in China and spread through trade routes, carried by fleas found on rodents. Rodents are most prevalent in cities, so these areas were hit the hardest. The disease passed to humans when the fleas would jump from the rats to a human host.

Every social group suffered from the Black Death—it was not a discriminating disease. But those who lived in rural settings were sometimes spared, as were the wealthy, who had less contact with outsiders and could afford to move to more secluded areas in an attempt to spare themselves.

The bubonic plague was a dreadful, fast-moving epidemic. Victims usually suffered from a high fever and had swelling under the armpits or in the groin. The buboes, or lymph nodes, would swell to the size of an egg. Those infected would often die within four or five days of contracting the plague.

The Black Death had many long-term consequences. Certain areas of Europe were nearly deserted in its aftermath, including some of its thriving cities. For example, Bremen, Germany, lost almost 7,000 of its 12,000 inhabitants; Florence, Italy, lost 40,000 of its nearly 90,000; and Paris lost more than 50,000 of its 180,000. Major cities had to create mass graveyards where the dead could be buried. European population only began to grow again in the last decades of the 15th century.

The Black Death also brought about economic changes. As large numbers of peasants died, there was a shortage of labor. Peasants had previously spent generations working for the same family, but after the plague hit, they began to take advantage of the labor shortages. Workers charged many times their usual rate for work and would sometimes move to a new lord or noble who offered better incentives and working conditions. In this way, the Black Death caused the landowning aristocracy to lose much of their power and status.

Answer the questions about the reading.

1. Number the events of the Black Plague in the correct order.

____ Landowning aristocracy began to lose power.
____ Victims died within several days.
____ Fleas began hosting on humans in Europe, infecting people there.
____ Victims' lymph nodes became swollen.
____ Fleas traveled on the bodies of rats to Europe via trade routes.

2. Where did the Black Death originate?

_____

3. Why do you think the plague may have been given the name Black Death?

_____

4. Was the Black Death a discriminating disease? Explain.

_____

5. The rat flea spread the plague. Can you think of another insect that can kill in such mass quantities? Explain.

_____

6. What was the effect of the plague on European cities?

_____

7. What was the effect of the plague on workers?

_____

_____

8. What was the effect of the plague on the wealthy?

_____

_____

9. Can you think of a modern medicine that could have helped prevent the devastating effects of the Black Death?

_____

10. If you lived in the 1340s, would you have wanted to live in the country or the city? Explain.

_____

_____

The Path of the Plague

The map below shows the spread of the bubonic plague through parts of Europe between 1347 and 1350.

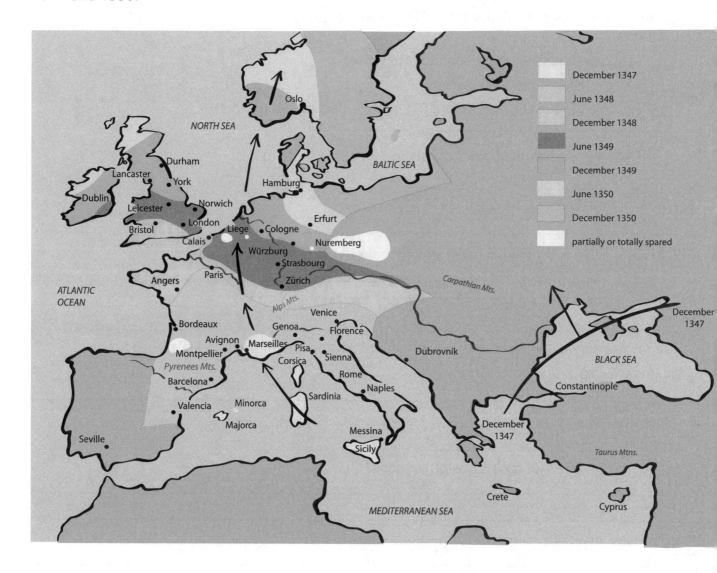

Answer the questions about the map.

1. According to the map, in what year did the Black Plague hit Sicily? _____

2. In what direction did the plague primarily move? _____

3. Across what body of water did the plague travel to get to Oslo, Norway?

_____

4. In what year did the plague strike Dublin, Ireland? _____

5. Did the plague strike London, England, before or after Dublin? _____

6. What do the light yellow areas indicate?

_____

7. What might be the reason these areas existed?

_____

8. Name two French cities hit by the plague that are shown on this map.

_____

9. Name one mountain range shown on this map.

_____

10. Why do you think the Black Death epidemic ended?

_____

_____

_____

Men of Honor

A knight was a mounted warrior of medieval Europe who served a king or other feudal superior, usually in return for land. Knighthood was taken quite seriously and had to be earned.

At about the age of eight, a boy would begin training in preparation for knighthood. This young trainee, known as a page, would train with mentors to learn about horses, armor, and weapons. Pages practiced fighting with a sword against a wooden stake and learned to skillfully use a bow and arrow. The lady of the castle taught a young page about manners and social graces, as well as how to sing, play instruments, and dance. A priest might give a page religious training and teach him to read and write.

By the age of fourteen, the page would become a squire. A squire was responsible for dressing a knight for battles and tournaments and taking care of the knight's armor and weapons. He would even follow his master on the battlefield to protect him if the knight fell.

A squire had to gain skill in using a lance, spear, or sword, so he would practice against a wooden dummy called a quintain. The quintain and a shield were hung on a wooden pole, and when hit, the whole structure would spin. The squire would learn to ride up and hit the shield's center, but then quickly move out of the way without getting hit and knocked off his horse by the quintain.

At about age twenty, a squire was finally prepared to be called a knight, which involved an extended ceremony. On the evening before becoming a knight, the squire confessed his sins to a priest, was given a symbolic bath, and then fasted in order to cleanse his soul. The squire would dress all in white and stay in a chapel all night praying and watching over his weapons and armor.

In the morning, the squire would dress in symbolically-colored clothing: red for his blood, white for purity, and brown for his return to the earth after death. At his induction, the knight swore a code of chivalry, which required him always to be brave, loyal, courteous, and to protect the defenseless. Knighthood was conferred by the overlord with an accolade, during which the new knight was tapped on the shoulders or neck with the flat side of the sword.

If this new knight ever broke his vows or acted dishonorably, he would be stripped of his knighthood in another ceremony, in which he was "buried." In the Middle Ages, a knight without honor was considered as good as dead.

Answer the questions about the reading.

1. Number the steps to knighthood in the correct order.

_____ page
_____ knight
_____ squire

2. What were two responsibilities of a squire?
_____
_____

3. What brave act did a squire have to perform?
_____
_____

4. How do you think you would feel if you had to perform this act?
_____

5. What are three things a page learned?
_____
_____

6. What is an accolade?
_____
_____

7. What did the clothes worn during an induction ceremony mean?
_____
_____

8. What did a squire have to do the night before being inducted as a knight?
_____
_____

9. What is chivalry?
_____
_____

10. If a knight were to betray the king, what do you think might happen?
_____

Shining Armor

Knights had to protect themselves during battle. In fact, they were so well protected that they depended on squires to keep their armor and weapons clean and in good working condition.

One of the earlier forms of armor was chain mail, which was made of small, metal rings. Thousands of rings were woven together to form an article of armor, such as a shirt, coif (cap), or leggings. Chain mail was heavy, uncomfortable, and made movement difficult. So, by the late 13th century, knights began wearing plated armor instead.

At first, plates were worn as a way to further protect only vital areas, such as the knight's chest and shoulders. But eventually knights were wearing plates all over their bodies, forming a full suit of plated armor. On their heads, knights wore a helmet with a metal visor to protect their faces. As you can imagine, full suits of plated armor were dreadfully hot, uncomfortable, and heavy. In fact, a suit of armor could weigh between 40 and 60 pounds!

To further protect themselves, knights carried a shield. Shields were made of either wood or metal, and were often decorated with a family emblem or crest. Knights also carried a weapon, often a sword, which weighed about 32 pounds. A sword was worn on the knight's left and was held in a casing fastened around his waist.

Not long after the development and use of the full suit of plate armor, it began to fall out of use. Weapons that utilized gunpowder became more common—and effective—and not even this full suit of metal could protect the knight from such powerful weaponry. Plate armor was cumbersome, and so once it was no longer serving its purpose, it was simply abandoned.

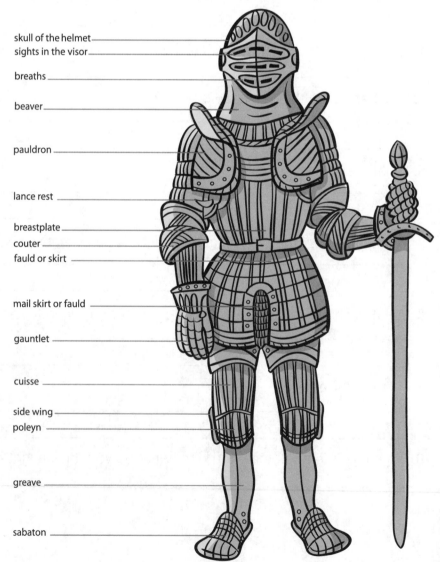

skull of the helmet
sights in the visor
breaths
beaver
pauldron
lance rest
breastplate
couter
fauld or skirt
mail skirt or fauld
gauntlet
cuisse
side wing
poleyn
greave
sabaton

Answer the questions about the reading.

1. Have you ever heard the phrase "a knight in shining armor"? What do you think it refers to?

_____

_____

2. What preceded plate armor? _____

3. Do you think it was labor intensive to make this type of armor? Explain.

_____

_____

4. What piece of plate armor covered a knight's lower leg? _____

5. What piece of plate armor covered a knight's elbow area? _____

6. What purpose do you think the breaths served for the knight?

_____

7. How much could a suit of armor and sword weigh altogether?_____

8. Did a knight need to be physically fit? Explain.

_____

_____

9. What piece of plate armor covered a knight's chest area? _____

10. What made plate armor became obsolete? _____

The Sword in the _____
NOUN

As you read the story, fill in each blank with any word from the correct part of speech. Have fun!

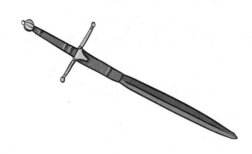

Centuries ago, there lived a(n) _____ King named _____.
LANGUAGE   NAME

The King had a(n) _____ named Arthur, but no one in _____ knew
OCCUPATION   PLACE

that Arthur _____. Arthur had been adopted by an _____ named
VERB (PAST TENSE)   NOUN

Sir Ector. When King Uther _____, there was great uproar. "_____!
VERB (PAST TENSE)   SILLY WORD

Who will be the next high king of Britain?" the _____ of the kingdom wondered.
PLURAL NOUN

One day, a(n) _____ stone appeared in the _____ of a
ADJECTIVE   PLACE

cathedral. Lodged in the _____ was a sword. The sword bore a(n)
NOUN

_____ : Whoever could _____ is the rightful _____
NOUN   VERB   OCCUPATION

of Britain. Many a local _____ tried to _____, but the sword would
NOUN   VERB

not budge from its place in the _____. _____ passed and the
NOUN   PLURAL NOUN

sword remained in its place. Arthur had _____ grown into a(n) _____
ADVERB   ADJECTIVE

man and happened upon the sword one day. Arthur grabbed the sword's _____ and
NOUN

_____. The sword released itself from the _____! Arthur gave the
VERB (PAST TENSE)   NOUN

sword to his brother _____ to use.
CELEBRITY MALE

Sir Ector saw _____'s sword and asked, "_____, where did
        SAME CELEBRITY MALE   OCCUPATION
you get that sword?" _____ said, "Arthur brought it to me, Father." Sir Ector asked
                     SAME CELEBRITY MALE
his adopted _____, "Arthur, where did you get this sword?"
            NOUN

Arthur _____, "I found it in a _____ in a nearby courtyard. It
       VERB (PAST TENSE)   NOUN
didn't _____ like it belonged to anyone."
       VERB

"_____, but it does belong to someone. It belongs to the next rightful
  EXCLAMATION
_____ of _____."
OCCUPATION   COUNTRY

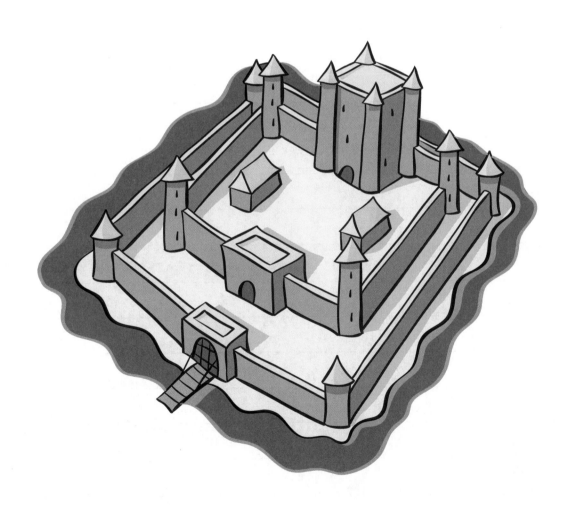

Your Own Arthurian Legend

You may have heard some of the dozens of stories about King Arthur. This body of material is often referred to as Arthurian Legend. Create a new story about King Arthur and write it on the lines below.

_____

_____

_____

_____

_____

_____

_____

_____

_____

_____

_____

_____

_____

_____

_____

_____

_____

_____

_____

_____

_____

_____

Serf for a Day

Pretend that you are a serf in the Middle Ages. What is your life like? What is your lord's name and what is he like? What is your home like? How are you treated? Does the Black Death come to your town? On the lines below, write a fictional first-person account from the point of view of a serf.

_____

_____

_____

_____

_____

_____

_____

_____

_____

_____

_____

_____

_____

_____

_____

_____

_____

Genetically Speaking

In most cells, including human cells, genetic information is organized into structures called chromosomes. Each chromosome contains hundreds—sometimes thousands—of smaller packages of information called genes, which perform functions such as telling your body to make your eyes brown and your hair curly, or to make your eyes green and your hair red.

Inherited traits are characteristics that are passed from parents to offspring. Because you come from two parents, each parent will provide one half of your genes for any trait through what are called alleles. You have two alleles for each gene, one from each parent. Individuals may inherit either two identical alleles or two different alleles from their parents.

Alleles are either dominant or recessive. A dominant allele is stronger, hence its name. Traits of dominant alleles are always observed, even when a recessive allele is present. But traits of recessive alleles are only observed when two recessive alleles are present.

Consider this example. The gene for the shape of your hairline has two alleles: widow's peak (W) or straight (w). The allele for widow's peak is dominant and the allele for straight hairline is recessive. The dominant allele is assigned a capital letter to show that it is stronger.

WW = Two widow's peak alleles (both dominant), resulting in a peaked hairline

Ww = One widow's peak allele (dominant) and one straight hairline allele (recessive), resulting in a peaked hairline

ww = Two straight hairline alleles (recessive), resulting in a straight hairline

Answer the questions about the reading.

1. What is inside a chromosome? _____

2. What purpose do genes serve? _____

3. What does the word *inherited* in paragraph 2 mean? Write the letter of the answer. ____
  a. received from a postal worker
  b. received from a peer
  c. received from a parent or ancestor by genetic transmission

4. What does a recessive trait do? Write the letter of the answer. ____
  a. produces its effect when combined with a contrasting allele
  b. produces no effect when combined with a contrasting allele
  c. produces its effect when combined with an identical chromosome

5. In a fight, who wins: a dominant allele or recessive allele? _____

If E represents the allele for an unattached earlobe (dominant trait) and e represents the allele for an attached earlobe (recessive trait), what happens to a person born with:

6. EE _____

7. Ee _____

8. ee _____

If R represents the allele for the ability to roll the tongue (dominant trait) and r represents the allele for the inability to do this (recessive trait), what happens to a person born with:

9. Rr _____

10. RR _____

11. rr _____

Mendel's Model

Gregor Johann Mendel is often called the father of genetics for his study of the inheritance of traits in pea plants. Mendel showed that the inheritance of traits follow particular laws, which were later named after him.

Mendel was born in Austria in 1822, and in 1847, he was ordained into the priesthood. Shortly thereafter it became apparent that he was suited to teaching. So in 1851, Mendel began attending the University of Vienna to train to be a teacher of mathematics and biology. There, he developed skills as a researcher, which he would later utilize.

Mendel did groundbreaking work in his study of the theories of heredity. Using simple pea plants, Mendel traced their seven basic characteristics and discovered three basic laws that governed the passage of a trait from one member of a species to another member of the same species.

Mendel's first law states that a sex cell of a plant will contain just one of two possible traits. His second law states that characteristics are inherited independently from another. Mendel's third law states that each inherited characteristic is determined by two hereditary factors, or genes, one from each parent. These decide whether a trait appears or not. Mendel's work and theories later became the model for the study of modern genetics, and are still recognized and used today.

Ironically, Mendel was not recognized for his work by his scientific peers. In fact, his work was relatively unappreciated until the turn of the 20th century. But Mendel's achievements were certainly revolutionary: his work led to the discovery of dominant and recessive traits, the concept of heterozygous and homozygous, and other advanced phenomena. Mendel died on January 6, 1884.

Answer the questions about the reading.

1. Who was Gregor Mendel?

_____

_____

2. What is his nickname? _____

3. What is Mendel's first law?

_____

_____

4. What is Mendel's second law?

_____

_____

5. What is Mendel's third law?

_____

_____

6. How did Mendel develop these laws?

_____

7. What does that tell you about the laws?

_____

8. What other groundbreaking facts did Mendel's work later reveal to the scientific world?

_____

_____

9. If an organism is homozygous, it might have RR or rr. What does this tell you?

_____

10. If an organism is heterozygous, it might have Rr. What does this tell you?

_____

Genetic Disorders

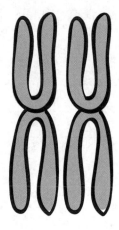

Genetic disorders are conditions that have some origin in an individual's genetic makeup. Many of these disorders are inherited and are governed by the same genetic rules that determine traits like hair color. They are either dominant genetic disorders or recessive genetic disorders.

Over 4,000 diseases are caused by genetic variants. But having a genetic mutation does not necessitate that a person actually develop that disease. You inherit one gene from each parent, therefore a normal gene can counteract a recessive, problematic gene.

But if the gene for a disease is dominant, or if the same recessive disease gene is present on both chromosomes in a pair, problems can arise. Those present through the first scenario are called dominant genetic disorders. If a person carries the dominant gene for a disease, he or she will usually have the disease and each of the person's children will have a 50% chance of inheriting the gene and developing the disease as well. Examples of this type of genetic disorder include achondroplasia, which is a form of dwarfism; Marfan syndrome, which is a connective tissue disorder; and Huntington's disease, which is a degenerative disease of the nervous system.

Other genetic disorders, such as cystic fibrosis, sickle cell anemia, and Tay-Sachs disease, are caused by recessive disease genes that a child inherits from both parents. They are called recessive gene disorders. When a person has just one recessive gene for a disease, that person is called a carrier. Carriers don't usually have the disease because they have a normal gene of that pair. Yet, when two carriers have a child together, the child has a 25% chance of developing the disease.

Answer the questions about the reading.

1. What is a genetic disorder?

_____

2. When a person has one recessive gene for a disease, he or she is called a carrier. *True* or *false*?

_____

3. Huntington's disease is a degenerative disease of the nervous system. *True* or *false*?

_____

4. If a person carries the dominant gene for a disease, he or she will usually not have the disease. *True* or *false*? _____

5. Achondroplasia is a connective tissue disorder. *True* or *false*? _____

6. A pair of dominant disease genes that a child inherits from both parents is called a recessive gene disorder. *True* or *false*? _____

7. When two carriers have a child together, the child has a 25% chance of developing the disease. *True* or *false*?_____

8. More than 40,000 diseases are caused by genetic variants. *True* or *false*?

_____

9. A normal gene can counteract a recessive, problematic gene. *True* or *false*?

_____

10. Can you think of another common genetic disorder that is caused by neither a recessive nor a dominant gene, but by a gene mutation?

_____

Periodically

The periodic table of the elements includes the types of elements that make up the universe and shows the relative properties of the atoms. The periodic table was invented by Dmitri I. Mendeleev and was later revised by Henry G. J. Moseley. Scientists and students use the periodic table to extract information about individual elements.

Elements are arranged from left to right and top to bottom, in order of increasing atomic number. Atomic number is the number of protons in the nucleus of an atom.

The different horizontal rows of elements are called periods. Each period groups elements by the highest energy level an electron in that element occupies in the unexcited state. The number of elements in a period increases as one moves down the periodic table.

The vertical columns in the periodic table are called groups. Each element shares common qualities with others in its group. For example, group 18 is the inert gases, which barely interact chemically with other elements.

Periodic Table of Elements

1																	18
1 H	2											13	14	15	16	17	2 He
3 Li	4 Be											5 B	6 C	7 N	8 O	9 F	10 Ne
11 Na	12 Mg	3	4	5	6	7	8	9	10	11	12	13 Al	14 Si	15 P	16 S	17 Cl	18 Ar
19 K	20 Ca	21 Sc	22 Ti	23 V	24 Cr	25 Mn	26 Fe	27 Co	28 Ni	29 Cu	30 Zn	31 Ga	32 Ge	33 As	34 Se	35 Br	36 Kr
37 Rb	38 Sr	39 Y	40 Zr	41 Nb	42 Mo	43 Tc	44 Ru	45 Rh	46 Pd	47 Ag	48 Cd	49 In	50 Sn	51 Sb	52 Te	53 I	54 Xe
55 Cs	56 Br	57 La*	72 Hf	73 Ta	74 W	75 Re	76 Os	77 Ir	78 Pt	79 Au	80 Hg	81 Tl	82 Pb	83 Bi	84 Po	85 At	86 Rn
87 Fr	88 Ra	89 Ac*	104 Rf	105 Ha	106 106	107 107	108 108	109 109	110 110								

✸ Lanthinide Series	58 Ce	59 Pr	60 Nd	61 Pm	62 Sm	63 Eu	64 Gd	65 Tb	66 Dy	67 Ho	68 Er	69 Tm	70 Yb	71 Lu
✸ Actinide Series	90 Th	91 Pa	92 U	93 Np	94 Pu	95 Am	96 Cm	97 Bk	98 Cf	99 Es	100 Fm	101 Md	102 No	103 Lr

Use the reading and table to answer the questions.

1. Underline the name of the first element on the periodic table.

    argon (Ar)   helium (He)   hydrogen (H)

2. What is its atomic number? ____

    1   2   3

3. Which two elements share some similar characteristics? Write the letter of the answer. ____

    a. silicon (Si) and magnesium (Mg)
    b. carbon (C) and magnesium (Mg)
    c. Silicon (Si) and carbon (C)

4. Which of these is **not** found in the earth's atmosphere? ____

    nitrogen (N)   gold (Au)   oxygen (O)

5. All of the following are in the same periods of the periodic table **except** ____. Circle the letter of the answer.

    a. sodium (Na), carbon (C), chlorine (Cl)
    b. beryllium (Be), oxygen (O), flourine (F)
    c. hydrogen (H), helium (He)

6. Sulfur's atomic number is ____.

7. The columns in the periodic table are called _____.

8. The rows in the periodic table are called _____.

9. The inventor of the periodic table was _____.

10. Why would a student, such as yourself, use the periodic table?

_____

_____

Anatomy of an Atom

Everything in the universe is composed of atoms, as they are the building blocks of the universe. Atoms are so small that millions of them would fit on the head of a pin, but what lies within them is even smaller still.

The center of an atom is called the nucleus. Though it contains nearly all of the mass of the atom, it occupies only a tiny fraction of the space inside the atom. The nucleus consists of particles called protons and neutrons that are tightly bound together. While neutrons are electrically neutral—hence their name—protons have a positive electric charge. An electrical charge is a force within the particle. It is also important to note that the number of protons in an atom determines its properties as an element.

Also found inside an atom are electrons, which are tiny, negatively charged particles that spin around the nucleus in special "orbits" called shells. They remain a great distance from the nucleus and are held in their shells by an electrical force. The protons and electrons of an atom are attracted to each other, like magnets, because of their opposite charges.

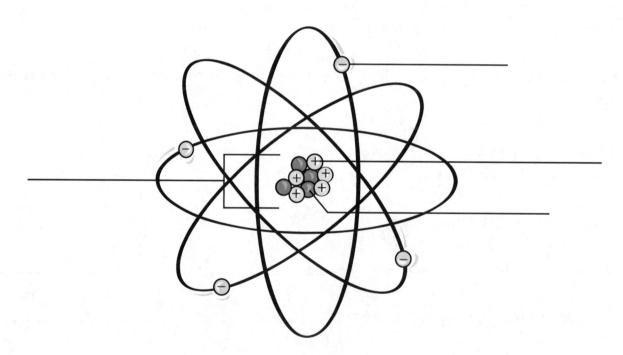

Follow the directions. Then use the reading to answer the questions.

1. Label a proton in the diagram.

2. Label an electron in the diagram.

3. Label the nucleus in the diagram.

4. Label a neutron in the diagram.

5. What charge do electrons have? _____

6. What charge do protons have? _____

7. What is the overall effect of this?

_____

8. Predict what might happen if protons had a negative electrical charge.

_____

_____

9. Where is most of the mass of an atom? _____

10. How are protons related to elements?

_____

_____

11. What is the proton number called when referring to the periodic table?

_____

Answer Key

Pages 6–7
1. possible answers: purebred, wealthy, prim, aloof, confident, narcissistic
2. possible answers: mutt, has new ideas, doesn't follow the status quo, humble
3. possible answers: idealistic, willing to take a chance, encouraging, supportive, purebred
4. The Wheaton Terrier says that he won't vote for Higgins because he can't expect Higgins to understand what purebreds want.
5. The Yorkipoo wants to know what Higgins stands for before he will vote for him.
6. The Shepherd-Labrador mix will vote for any mutt that runs.
7. Answers will vary.
8. possible answer: They seem nice for the dogs, but they also seem unrealistic.
9. She is overly confident that she will still win, because Purebreds always win and she has made some irresistible promises.
10. possible answer: Yes, it seems like a U.S. presidential election. Some voters follow the candidate who is just like them, others just want change, and others want to understand both sides before they can make a choice.

Pages 8–9
1. It promises free treats. It probably will draw voters – at least the ones who want a snack.
2. No, because it's not likely that dogs will never have to wear a leash.
3. superiority
4. c
5. It means that Higgins will be a change from the type of administration that is typically in place.
6. Answers will vary.
7. Answers will vary.
8. to sway voters' opinions
9. Answers will vary.
10. possible answers: Bush, Adams, Roosevelt, Harrison, Kennedy

Page 10
Fliers will vary, but should express specific viewpoints or slogans.

Page 11
1. Answers will vary, but two candidates will likely be one

Republican and one Democrat.
2. Answers will vary.
3. If a candidate has more pros, then he or she is likely the better choice. If a candidate has more cons, then he or she is likely not the best choice. This exercise can help a person decide whom to vote for.
4. Answers will vary.
5. Yes; answers will vary, but could be a member of the Green party or Libertarian party, among others.
6. He or she was not a member of the Democratic or Republican two-party system. Most electoral voters and the media support and publicize only members of these parties.
7. possible answers: It shows that we have a two-party system. This can be good because uncommon and unconventional ideas remain non-influential, so policies and governments do not change rapidly. This enhances stability while eventually allowing for ideas that gain favor to become politically influential. This can be bad because two-way elections encourage people to run negative campaigns. If one of the two parties becomes weak, a single, dominant party system could develop.

Pages 12–13
1. elephant
2. Answers will vary.
3. donkey
4. Answers will vary.
5. Thomas Nast
6. Harper's Weekly
7. 1870, 1874
8. Andrew Jackson
9. Answers will vary.
10. Answers will vary.

Pages 14–15
1. holding Election Day on a weekend would not be better than on a Tuesday
2. Answers will vary.
3. Answers will vary.
4. to inform, to persuade
5. severe, stormy
6. never, always
7. 1845
8. possible answers: As of November, the fall harvest was over; in most parts of the country, the weather was still mild enough to permit voters to travel without fear of inclement weather; Tuesday

was the first day of the week when people could complete the long-distance travel; November 1 was already All Saint's Day and the day of the month that merchants traditionally reserved for balancing their books and taking inventory.
9. For working Americans, weekends are a designated time for family obligations and errands, as well as recreational activities, so voters are just as unlikely to find time to vote on a Saturday or Sunday as on a Tuesday.
10. Answers will vary.

Pages 16–17
1. photosynthesis; chloroplast
2. It wouldn't have any food and couldn't survive.
3. cell wall, vacuole
4. mitosis
5. cell membrane
6. possible answers: Rough ER is covered with ribosomes that give it a rough appearance; smooth ER buds off from rough ER, moving the newly made proteins and lipids to the Golgi body and membranes.
7. lysosome

Pages 18–19
1. A
2. P
3. P
4. B
5. A
6. B
7. lysosome
8. nucleus
9. vacuole
10. mitochondria

Pages 20–21
1. very tiny
2. one cell
3. Because they only have one cell, they are "solitary" or "alone."
4. bacterium
5. If something is aerobic, it needs atmospheric oxygen to live. If something is anaerobic, it can use oxygen from other molecular compounds.
6. Bacteria cells lack a nucleus and other membrane-bound organelles, except ribosomes. Unlike animals and plants, bacteria have pili, flagella, and most have a cell capsule. Bacteria cells are the entire organism, while plant and animal cells are just a tiny part

of the organism.
7. Yes, they are everywhere.
8. swift, hardy, robust, useful, hazardous
9. Bacteria cause illness, and they can survive conditions that would kill most other organisms. In the right conditions, bacteria develop a thick outer wall and enter a dormant phase, thereby protecting themselves from harm, and so we need to clean with strong chemicals.
10. rotting flesh, such as a dead animal

Pages 22–23
1. to inform
2. _5_ Jefferson died on July 4, 1826, at the age of eighty three.
   _2_ Jefferson was also a member of the Continental Congress and chosen in 1776 to draft the Declaration of Independence.
   _1_ Jefferson was born in Albemarle County, Virginia, on April 13, 1743.
   _3_ As president, Jefferson purchased the Louisiana Territory and supported the Lewis and Clark Expedition.
   _4_ He sold his collection of books to the government to form the core of the Library of Congress.
3. a person who has wide interests and is expert in several areas
4. The following should be underlined: University of Virginia
5. architect, president, inventor, lawyer
6. having made rich or richer by adding some desirable quality
7. On that date, Jefferson died at the age of eighty-three, John Adams passed away, and the country was celebrating the fiftieth anniversary of the signing of the Declaration of Independence.
8. possible answers: George Washington, James Madison, Patrick Henry, John Adams
9. Monticello
10. He purchased the Louisiana Territory and supported the Lewis and Clark Expedition.

Pages 24–25
1. exploratory

2. Its main goal was to locate a route that would allow for America to expand westward.
3. Missouri
4. Pacific Ocean
5. false
6. Missouri River
7. 8,000 miles
8. b
9. journey, voyage, trip
10. opinion

Pages 26–27
1.

May 14, 1804 — The Corps of Discovery begins its journey up the Missouri River.
November 4, 1804 — Lewis and Clark hire Toussaint Charbonneau and Sacagawea to act as guides and interpreters.
August 12, 1805 — Lewis discovers that there is no Northwest Passage.
August 17, 1805 — The main party arrives at the Shoshone camp, where Sacagawea recognizes the chief as her brother.
March 23, 1806 — The team sets out for home.

2. There was no Northwest Passage.
3. It is surprising, since the trip was long and grueling, with bad weather and scarce resources at times.
4. Thomas Jefferson
5. She acted as a guide and interpreter, and she saved possessions nearly lost.
6. Answers will vary.

Pages 28–29
1. F, T, T, F
2. communicate
3. A single receiving neuron has thousands of receptor sites and may receive many different messages at once.
4. soma
5. neurotransmitters
6. gray matter
7. Dendrites are "tree-like" because they branch out from the body of the cell, like branches on a tree.
8. c
9. a
10. b

Pages 30–31
1.

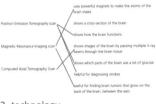

Positron Emission Tomography scan — uses powerful magnets to make the atoms of the brain shake / shows a cross-section of the brain / shows how the brain functions
Magnetic Resonance Imaging scan — shows images of the brain by passing multiple X-ray beams through the brain tissue / shows which parts of the brain use a lot of glucose / helpful for diagnosing strokes
Computed Axial Tomography Scan — useful for finding brain tumors that grow on the back of the brain, between the ears

2. technology
3. normal
4. PET
5. MRI

Pages 32–33
1. North American plate
2. The author describes how a sheet of ice cracks apart.
3. lithosphere
4. possible answers: earthquakes, volcanoes, oceanic trenches, mountain range formation,

many other geologic phenomena
5. Antarctic plate
6. Earth is like an onion with many layers beneath its surface.
7. 14
8. A mountain range would form.
9. c
10. An earthquake would occur.

Pages 34–35
1.

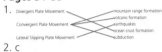

Divergent Plate Movement
Convergent Plate Movement
Lateral Slipping Plate Movement
— mountain range formation
— volcano formation
— earthquakes
— ocean crust formation
— subduction

2. c
3. expanded
4. a. divergent
   b. convergent
   c. lateral
5. convergent plate movement
6. convergent plate movement
7. divergent plate movement
8. lateral slipping plate movement

Pages 36–37
1. opinion
2. fact
3. fact
4. opinion
5. Greenland; He studied it as a child and went on expeditions there.
6. meteorology
7. possible answer: He had an immense interest in science; he liked to learn, as evidenced by the many branches he studied and degrees he earned; he was experimental and brave for trying new things; he was curious and wanted to understand complex ideas.
8. Pangaea was a supercontinent consisting of all of earth's landmasses.
9. It got the name "All-earth" because it consisted of "all" of earth.
10. possible answers: He likely felt that others didn't understand him or his ideas; he probably felt afraid that perhaps he was wrong, but he persevered.

Pages 38–39
Stories will vary.
1. A fool and his money are soon parted.
2. The early bird gets the worm.
3. Look before you leap.
4. You made your bed, so now you have to lie in it.
5. Answers will vary, but might include phrases such as: A stitch in time saves nine. A rolling stone gathers no moss. The squeaky wheel gets the oil. Beware of wolves in sheep's clothing. Every cloud has a silver lining.

Pages 40–41
1. a network of people working

secretly to help fugitive slaves escape to the north and to Canada
2. for many years before and during the Civil War
3. possible answers: brave, motivated, determined
4. possible answers: brave, supportive, forward thinking, risk-taking
5. possible answers: supportive, forward-thinking
6. possible answers: Harriet Tubman, John Fairfield, Levi Coffin
7. No, it was not an actual railroad. It was a network of people.
8. Quakers
9. George Washington
10. possible answers: Cincinnati, Ohio; Wilmington, Delaware; Detroit, Michigan; Sandusky, Ohio; Erie, Pennsylvania; Buffalo, New York.

Pages 42–43

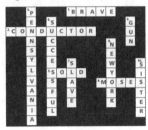

Pages 44–45
1. a slave named Henrietta; She is brave and tired of being held captive, so she wants to escape.
2. She feels that it tastes bitter and wants to escape to seek a better life in the North.
3. She is frightened and unsure. She worries that she'll get caught.
4. She is excited and relieved to be free. She feels indebted to those who helped her.
5. possible answers: long, arduous, scary, tiring, grueling
6. Harriet Tubman
7. Susan B. Anthony
8. that it's a safehouse for slaves
9. Maryland; Canada
10. Answers will vary.

Page 46
Stories will vary.

Page 47
Stories will vary.

Pages 48–49
1. _2_ African slaves were given meager ingredients, so they developed their own style of food.

_1_ Africans were brought from Africa, along with African ingredients.

_3_ The African slave style of cooking became popular and is now called soul food.
2. The author feels that it was a dark time in our history.
3. The following should be underlined: The term *soul food* is now commonly used to describe a style of food that originated during a dark time in the history of the United States. While the origins of soul food aren't pleasant, the result was a special blending of African and American culinary styles, producing food that is vibrant and rich in character.
4. the South
5. rice, okra, yams, peanuts, and black-eyed peas
6. possible answer: deep frying, barbecue
7. a type of pancake prepared by boiling water and stirring in flour and other ingredients
8. dried kernels of Indian corn
9. meager, scanty, scraps, leftovers, measly, paltry, undesirable, discarded
10. Answers will vary.

Pages 50–51
1. B
2. C
3. P
4. C
5. P
6. P
7. B
8. P
9. The dough would get stiff. The biscuits would be dense.
10. They would be too thick, so they would not cook fast enough inside.

Pages 52–53
1. The Emancipation Proclamation is now viewed as a milestone in the path to ending slavery.
2. formal withdrawal from an organization
3. The Emancipation Proclamation confirmed that the Civil War was now a war about ending slavery—a war of freedom.
4. possible answers: hopeful, excited, relieved, like someone was on my side
5. President Abraham Lincoln
6. possible answers: It didn't apply to the loyal border states; it exempted parts of the Confederacy that had already come under Union control; the freedom it promised depended upon Union military victory.
7. almost 200,000
8. Those who had previously been slaves could now fight in the war to make their peers free as well.

9. He hoped to inspire all blacks, and in particular, slaves in the Confederacy, to support the Union cause and to keep England and France from giving political recognition and military aid to the Confederacy.
10. excused; released from a requirement; not applied to

Pages 54–55
1. primary
2. It presents information in its original form, not interpreted, condensed, or evaluated by other writers.
3. September 22, 1862
4. It applied only to states that had seceded from the Union.
5. The following should be underlined: …by virtue of the power in me vested as Commander-In-Chief of the Army and Navy of the United States in time of actual armed rebellion against the authority and government of the United States.
6. possible answers: favorably, positively
7. possible answers: negatively, with anger
8. the Constitution
9. The following should be underlined: And I hereby enjoin upon the people so declared to be free to abstain from all violence, unless in necessary self defense; and I recommend to them that, in all cases when allowed, they labor faithfully for reasonable wages.
10. A.D. means Anno Domini, which indicates that something has taken place in the Common Era, as opposed to B.C., or Before Christ.

Pages 56–57
1. This letter is to Mr. Mario Lasky, Superintendent of Schools, because the school district is considering lengthening the school day.
2. a parent or teacher
3. She is in disagreement with the idea of lengthening the school day.
4. Yes, she offers several significant, logical reasons to support her opinion.
5. Answers will vary.
6. Answers will vary.
7. beneficial
8. a
9. to remain uninvolved
10. a

Pages 58–59
1. The processes affecting earth today are the same ones that affected it in the past.
2. Structural geologists carefully observe and interpret layers of

rock. They study the way earth's crust is deformed by mountain-building processes.
3. to inform
4. true
5. false
6. true
7. true
8. false
9. The bottom layers are the oldest.
10. They formed from lava cooling after a volcanic eruption.

Pages 60–61
1. a list of earth's life forms from youngest to oldest
2. Tertiary
3. Fossils older than the Cambrian Period are rare.
4. dragonfly
5. Mesozoic

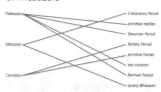

Pages 62–63

Pages 64–65
1. Answers will vary.
2. dinosaur-blood, a condition that combines certain aspects of warm-bloodedness with a changing metabolism over the animal's lifetime
3. An asteroid that hit the earth at the end of the Cretaceous Period may have caused the dinosaur extinction. But some dinosaur specialists claim that dinosaurian diversity was already in decline by the end of the Cretaceous, and the asteroid impact may have been the straw that broke the camel's back.
4. more than 150 million years
5. the act of preying
6. a
7. idiom

Pages 66–67
1. _4_ Assemble DNA into chromosomes.
   _1_ Find complete, intact DNA of the species.
   _7_ Keep baby dinosaur alive in a world full of germs and other dangers to which it would have no resistance.
   _6_ "Raise" egg under the optimal conditions for that species' development.
   _5_ Implant chromosomes into a compatible, living, intact egg.

_2_ Extract DNA from its source.
   _3_ Sequence DNA to uncover the genetic code of the dinosaur.
2. possible answer: Jurassic Park, among others
3. Based on the reading, it could not happen.
4. Answers will vary.
5. They are extinct and that is a permanent condition.

Page 68
Answers will vary, but should express a definite opinion and supporting reasons for that opinion.

Page 69
Letters will vary, but should be written in proper business-letter format and be convincing.

Pages 70–71
Descriptions and maps will vary widely, but should address all the questions posed and beyond.

Pages 72–73
1. Megaraptor, Deinonychus, or Utahraptor
2. Micropachycephalosaurus, or others
3. Hypselosaurus
4. Ankylosaurus
5. Hadrosaurus
6. Pentaceratops
7. Deinocheirus
8. Minmi and Khaan
9. Unenlagia
10. Sauropod

Pages 74–75
1. d
2. a
3. b
4. a person who starts a new business enterprise
5. the people who traveled to California in 1849 in search of gold; a member of the football team
6. the goal of material prosperity available to all who seek it
7. taking advantage of an opportunity, often with little regard for the circumstances
8. television ads, magazine ads, Internet, sweepstakes/prizes
9. Answers will vary, but could include: new technology, such as MP3 players and televisions, celebrities
10. 1848

Pages 76–77
1. Neither option was easy or pleasurable.
2. Answers will vary.
3. The Panama Canal did not exist yet, so there was no shortcut.
4. possible answers: At the Pacific side, they sometimes

waited there for weeks or even months for another ship; when a ship finally did arrive, passage might cost $500 or $1,000— an extraordinary amount of money at the time; sometimes there was no space, even if a traveler had the funds; many of the ships on the Pacific side of the voyage were not sea worthy and sank en route.
5. Answers will vary.
6. possible answers: This journey could take them six months; they encountered Native Americans for the first time, whom they feared; many of those journeying didn't prepare well enough for the trip and water was either spoiled or in short supply.
7. Porter planned to fly people west on propeller-driven balloons powered by steam engines. No, the contraption never lifted off the ground.
8. Answers will vary, but should reflect that it wasn't a pleasurable trip for anyone, even children.
9. inflation
10. Answers will vary, but could include: oil, prime real estate, diamonds, precious metals, "fad" toys such as video game systems

Pages 78–79
1. For many, travel by ship was too costly an option.
2. Many were in covered wagons, many rode horses, and still many others simply walked the distance.
3. They endured violent thunderstorms and torrential rain that turned the land into a massive mud hole. They also suffered through scorching heat. Also, sunscreen wasn't invented yet, so those who survived the journey suffered from dry, sun-baked skin for months.
4. disease
5. unsanitary
6. Answers will vary.
7. Answers will vary.
8. exhausted, thirsty, famished
9. fresh
10. Yes, packs of wagons would pass each day, causing wagon "traffic."

Pages 80–81
1.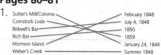
2. Nevada
3. Las Vegas
4. Over time, inflation makes a dollar worth less and less.

5. Europe
6. 1.5 million dollars
7. members of the Church of Jesus Christ of Latter-day Saints
8. The gold rush was drying up. The gold had mostly been found and mined by that point.

Page 82
Answers will vary, but should include forms of food and water, clothing, cleaning/grooming supplies

Page 83
Drawn routes and paragraphs will vary.

Pages 84–85
1. the gold rush
2. He became the inventor of the blue jean.
3. probably not; although, like other gold-seekers headed toward California, he was dreaming big
4. miners
5. almost everyone
6. Blue denim is called *genes* in French, which became *jeans* in English.
7. Jacob Davis
8. Davis didn't have the money to patent this process, so he suggested that Strauss and he take out the patent together.
9. Levi Strauss's invention has become an international phenomenon and an icon of American culture.
10. Answers will vary.

Pages 86–87
1. a newspaper
2. opinions and editorials, or opposite (next to) the editorial page
3. to persuade
4. That humans have been detrimental; the author is passionate that humans are harming the Everglades.
5. The following should be underlined: negative, extremel evident, pollution, indiscriminate hunting, extinction
6. to make readers think
7. South Florida Research Center's research into how changes occurring outside the parks affect the delicate areas within their boundaries may lead to a brighter future for many species. Legislation such as the Endangered Species Act of 1973 provides for the classification of wildlife species as "endangered" or "threatened," and authorizes legal protection of species listed.
8. You can become informed on the status of plants and wildlife in Florida and support conservation legislation. You can also be proactive by

opting not to purchase products that come from endangered or threatened plant or wildlife species in addition to reporting those who are known dealers of endangered or threatened plants and wildlife.
9. to keep safe from injury, harm, or destruction
10. An effect is something that happens because of a cause; To affect is to produce an effect

Pages 88–89
1.
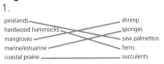

2. eight
3. Slight changes in elevation, salinity, and soil throughout this park have resulted in different environments.
4. mangrove forest
5. pinelands
6. freshwater marl prairies and freshwater sloughs

Pages 90–91

A	M	E	R	I	C	A	N	C	R	O	C	O	D	I	L
M	O	E	G	D	I	S	S	E	C	T	E	G	O	F	D	S	E
O	E	C	L	A	T	I	O	N	A	L	P	A	R	K	X	M	W	G
O	X	N	A	C	A	F	I	F	O	S	S	I	L	O	C	Z	I
S	L	O	R	I	D	A	P	A	N	H	E	B	L	J	S
E	M	M	O	R	T	A	L	E	E	R	Y	G	M	D	U
V	N	L	T	S	O	L	S	T	F	P	U	K	I	F	T	A
L	T	A	M	F	C	H	U	Z	G	I	A	A	T	J	C	L
E	C	V	O	S	N	O	A	G	M	T	M	E	S	S	R	L
J	B	N	I	U	O	A	R	G	D	L	W	A	E	C	H	A	O
D	T	I	S	L	A	V	I	E	Q	E	E	L	R	S	I	G
F	A	T	H	E	R	O	F	E	V	E	R	G	L	A	D	E

Pages 92–93
1. false
2. false
3. true
4. true
5. run fast and straight away from the alligator
6. No, it can see you, and could attack.
7. birds
8. No, the barrier is not high enough to make it safe. Alligators can climb over fences.
9. No, it is dangerous and illegal.
10. reptiles

Pages 94–95
1. Ireland
2. Saint Patrick, the patron saint of Ireland
3. worldwide
4. annually on March 17
5. It is the anniversary of Saint Patrick's death in the 5th century.
6. not overtly religious
7. to give relief for a time
8. adults taking a break from Lent and drinking a pint of ale
9. The government of Ireland established the St. Patrick's Day Festival.
10. Answers will vary, but could include shamrocks,

leprechauns, green, beer, parades, music, corned beef and cabbage, Irish soda bread.

Pages 96–97
1. the patron saint of Ireland
2. Patrick was born in Britain near the end of the 4th century. This is ironic because he is Ireland's most beloved saint, yet he wasn't Irish, and because the Irish and British have historically been at odds.
3. Not really; Patrick's father was a Christian deacon, but he may have taken the role because of tax incentives, rather than out of devotion to his religion.
4. converting the Irish to Christianity
5. He banished all the snakes from Ireland.
6. Most Irish practiced a nature based pagan religion. Their culture centered around oral legend and myth. The Irish were accustomed honoring their gods with fire.
7. 2, 6, 5, 4, 1, 3
8. Saint Patrick is the patron saint of Ireland and one of Christianity's most widel known figures.
9. biography
10. possible answers: Yes, because he tried to meld their beliefs with his, rather than eradicate their beliefs. No, because he still tried to convert them to a different religion.

Pages 98–99
1. __1__ Spray 8-inch-diameter cake pan with nonstick spray.
   __3__ Using floured hands, shape dough into ball.
   __5__ Cool bread in pan 10 minutes before serving.
   __4__ Transfer to buttered pan and flatten slightly.
   __2__ Whisk together flour, 4 tablespoons sugar, baking powder, salt, and baking soda in a large bowl.
2. 19th century
3. It was probably one of their first foods to use baking soda.
4. to divide the loaf into quarters
5. It could get lumpy and not blend well.
6. milk, orange juice, lemon, eggs, water

Pages 100–101
1. Great Potato Famine
2. A disease infected the potato crop, which was their main food source. They were all starving to death.
3. Answers will vary, but could include feeling scared, uncertain, homesick, but excited for the future and to be in a new

place.
4. They did not receive a warm welcome. Americans scorned the Irish for their religious beliefs and found their accents repugnant.
5. Answers will vary, but could include feeling scared, uncertain, homesick, confused, angry.
6. The Irish realized that they could use their great numbers as political power.
7. the Irish voting block
8. Green is the token color of Ireland, and there were so many Irish voting, that they were very influential, like a machine.
9. President Harry Truman attended the New York City St. Patrick's Day parade. It was a proud moment for the many Irish whose ancestors had to fight stereotypes and racial prejudice to find acceptance in America.
10. John Fitzgerald Kennedy, a famine descendent, became the thirty-fifth President of the United States. In little more than a century, Irish-Americans had moved from the position of the despised all the way to the Oval Office.

Pages 102–103
1. Irish colonists
2. Boston, Massachusetts
3.

1961	pounds of green vegetable dye released into the Chicago River the first time
1766	participants in the New York City parade procession
150,000+	year in which several New York Irish aid societies decided to unite their parades to form just one New York City St. Patrick's Day Parade
1848?	year in which it was realized that the Chicago River could be dyed green
100+	year in which the first official parade in New York City was held

4. No, because they were testing for sewage leakage!
5. Because St. Patrick's Day was a religious holiday in Ireland
6. principal, main
7. In order to minimize environmental damage, only forty pounds of dye are used.
8. several hours
9. It turns orange!
10. Answers will vary.

Pages 104–105
1. something that stands for or suggests something else
2. a popular belief or tradition that has grown around something or someone
3. Perhaps the only one that does is the belief that he used a shamrock to explain the Christian trinity.
4. an object, activity, or idea used in place of another to suggest a likeness or analogy between them
5. The Irish used their shamrock as a symbol of nationalism to demonstrate their displeasure with English rule.
6. Irish culture has a rich

tradition of myths, legends, and storytelling. Tales were passed down from one generation to the next, usually orally.
7. Stories gain new details but sometimes lose their truth in the process.
8. blue
9. Answers will vary.
10. Legends will vary.

Page 106
Answers will vary, but should reflect the indicated part of speech.

Page 107
Descriptions and drawings will vary.

Pages 108–109
1. wail
   keen
   gaelic
   folklore
   spirit
   death
   lament
   mourner
2. c
3. a female spirit whose appearance warns a family that one of them will soon die
4. She usually appears as a beautiful, young woman, a majestic matron, or a disheveled, old hag. She wears either a grey, hooded cloak or the winding sheet, or grave robe, of the dead.
5. Depending on the area of Ireland in which she is seen, the banshee can be screaming, singing, or wailing.
6. possible answer: I would feel scared that someone I know was going to die—or even that I was going to die!
7. washerwoman; Gaelic
8. King James I of Scotland; the banshee foretold his murder

Pages 110–111
1. Celtic lands
2. Samhain; "summer's end"
3. costumes, ghosts, bobbing for apples
4. ghosts of the dead
5. a
6. The Celts believed that the presence of the otherworldly spirits on Samhain enhanced the Celtic priests' ability to make predictions about the future, such as how long the coming winter would be.
7. Answers will vary.
8. Romans, Christians
9. about 2,000 years old
10. So they could reignite them later. When the celebration was over, they would reignite their hearth fires using fire from the sacred bonfire. They believed this ritual would

protect them during the coming winter.

Pages 112–113
1. Ireland
2. Cork is about six miles southeast of Blarney, and is Ireland's second largest city, after Dublin.
3. a block of stone built into the battlements of Blarney Castle
4. Dermot McCarthy, King of Munster; 1446
5. You will be forever endowed with the gift of gab.
6. Probably not—it's a folktale.
7. This tradition dates back to Queen Elizabeth I supposedly saying, "This is all Blarney. What he says he rarely means," about McCarthy, who didn't seem to want to discuss her taking over the castle.
8. Answers will vary, but could include the Statue of Liberty, Ellis Island, the White House, the Alamo, Mount Rushmore, presidential homes, Civil War battlegrounds, etc.
9. the harbor town of Dun Laoghaire, where she will visit the James Joyce Tower
10. a form of farewell; Gaelic

Pages 114–115
1. Y
2. J
3. N
4. J
5. B
6. Y
7. J
8. Y
9. B
10. The Irish were always storytellers: even before the written word, they would pass down stories orally. This could have led to a desire for writing.

Pages 116–117
1. poetry
2. William Butler Yeats
3. 1892
4. The poet declares that he will arise and go to the lake island called Innisfree.
5. It's a place with a small cabin "of clay and wattles made." There he will have nine bean rows and a beehive, and live alone in the glade loud with the sound of bees.
6. He finds it peaceful there.
7. The following should be underlined: midnight's all a-glimmer; evening full of the linnet's wings
8. soothing
9. to the city, or a more urban place
10. It's worse to him. Even when he is in the city, the author continues to hear the sounds

of nature that he loves from the lake isle of Innisfree.

Pages 118–119

Pages 120–121
1. title-down poetry
2. haiku
3. list poetry
4. alphabet poetry
5. terse verse
6. limerick

Page 122
Poems will vary.

Page 123
Answers will vary.

Pages 124–125
1. true
2. true
3. false
4. true
5. true
6. false
7. Robert Frost
8. four
9. four; quatrain
10. eight

Pages 126–127
1. mesosphere
2. c
3. ionosphere
4. stratosphere
5. ionosophere
6. The follwoing should be underlined: water vapor, carbon dioxide, methane, nitrous oxide, and others
7. tropopause
8. stratosphere
9. Yes, the ozone molecules absorb ultraviolet radiation from the sun and protect us from its harmful effects. Its maintenance is crucial for our survival.
10. Answers will vary, but could include the fact there is a growing "hole" in the ozone caused by pollution.

Pages 128–129
1. b
2. stratosphere
3. filtering the sun's UV rays
4. the polar regions
5. Aurora
6. The leading industrial countries agreed to stop using CFCs.
7. CFCs linger in the troposphere for years before reaching the stratosphere and the ozone layer.

8. the situation would be a lot worse today
9. c
10. a

Pages 130–131
1. inform, persuade
2. It makes you think of water as the victim of pollution, rather than the cause.
3. faraway places such as France, Iceland, or Maine
4. Delivering bottled water burns fossil fuels and results in the release of thousands of tons of harmful emissions. Since some bottled water is also shipped or stored cold, electricity is expended for refrigeration.
5. Possibly, as chemicals in plastic bottles may leach into the water.
6. Americans
7. Recycling just one can save enough energy to power a 60 watt light bulb for six hours.
8. carpeting or fleece clothing
9. The author admits that old pipes and outdated treatment threaten tap water quality. Yes, this seems opposite of the author's general argument that people should drink from the tap, rather than from bottles.
10. By admitting that tap water can be dangerous, but still offering a solution, the author has actually made the argument more persuasive.

Pages 132–133
1. Harry Potter
2. Lord Voldemort
3. J. K. Rowling
4. Harry as a schoolboy and Harry as a wizard
5.

Harry Potter and the Sorcerer's Stone	2000
Harry Potter and the Chamber of Secrets	1999
Harry Potter and the Half-Blood Prince	2007
Harry Potter and the Goblet of Fire	1998
Harry Potter and the Order of the Phoenix	2005
Harry Potter and the Prisoner of Azkaban	2003
Harry Potter and the Deathly Hallows	1999

6. Rowling does not avoid serious or frightening topics in her writing. The Harry Potter series depicts everything from self-sacrifice to death, which has enabled the books to successfully cross the boundary between adults' and children's books.
7. Answers will vary.
8. Answers will vary.
9. Answers will vary, but could include the opinion that they are based on the occult.
10. Answers will vary.

Pages 134–135
1. Diagon Alley is a street containing an assortment of shops and restaurants for wizards.

2. London, England
3. tapping the right brick in the wall behind the Leaky Cauldron
4. Knockturn Alley
5. 2
6. cauldron shop
7. Quality Quidditch Supplies
8. Magical Menagerie
9. Magical Menagerie or Eeylops Owl Emporium
10. Florean Fortescue's Ice Cream Parlor

Pages 136–137
1. Joanne Kathleen Rowling
2. so that her gender would be unknown
3. welfare
4. worried, sad, determined to make it
5. relieved, honored, fulfilled
6. 3, 1, 4, 5, 2
7. It was rejected.
8. Answers will vary, but many people would feel sad, rejected, unaccomplished, or as though they weren't good enough.

Pages 138–139
1. 3, 4, 2, 5, 1
2. permeated or influenced by
3. engorgement charm
4. It makes a person's tongue swell up to ten times its normal size.
5. It would be hard to break apart.
6. $1\frac{1}{4}$ pounds
7. b
8. 9 x 12 inches
9. The candy could stick to it.
10. milk, eggs, nuts, baking powder, brown sugar

Pages 140–141
1. Transfiguration
2. Arithmancy
3. Divination
4. Dark Arts
5. Herbology
6. Charms
7. Legilimency
8. Occlumency
9. Charms
10. Occlumency

Page 142
Answers will vary.

Page 143
Spells will vary.

Pages 144–145
1. Seeker
2. brooms
3. by catching the Golden Snitch
4. by throwing the Quaffle through the other team's hoops or by catching the Golden Snitch
5. six
6. The Goalie's job is to protect the three hoops so that the other team cannot score.

7. 150
8. Beaters protect their teammates by ensuring that the Bluggers are always heading toward the other team.
9. Answers will vary.
10. Answers will vary.

Pages 146–147
1. Sleep deprivation has numerous negative effects, so receiving enough Zs is vital for young people.
2. c
3. having lost something or never received something important
4. one hour more each night
5. true
6. false
7. true
8. to make slow or difficult the progress of
9. allows people to fall asleep
10. Answers will vary.

Pages 148–149
1. morning
   sleeping environment
   sleep hygiene
   caffeine
   exercise
2. Your sleep pattern would be very thrown off.
3. sleepy
4. overly awake from exercising too late
5. Generally, not that well! Sleep patterns are usually poor for those who do not exercise.
6. Your system would be very stimulated by the caffeine and lights and you wouldn't be able to fall asleep.

Page 150
Letters will vary, but should use proper business letter format, clearly state an opinion, provide supporting reasons, and offer a course of action.

Page 151
Descriptions or drawings will vary.

Pages 152–153
1. Answers will vary.
2. Scientists do not really understand how El Niño forms.
3. Yes, because it causes major weather changes, potentially flooding and drought, and is changing the temperatures of the oceans.
4. "The Little Boy": ;South American fisherman gave it the name El Niño, a Spanish term for "The Little Boy," because they noticed it often happening around Christmastime, when Christ was born.
5. It usually occurs once every 4 years and lasts for about 18

months at a time.
6. volatile
7. c
8. No, they can only study it and try to predict it.
9. possible answers: warmer sea temperatures, drought, flood.
10. possible answers: global warming, melting polar ice caps

Pages 154–155

Pages 156–157
1. having a classification according to rank
2. Carolus Linnaeus
3. a scientist who studies the branch of biology dealing with plant life
4. Latin
5. a scientist who studies the general principles of scientific classification
6. Scientists might have to rearrange the current classification scheme, adding this new species and moving other species from one genus to another.
7. following in order
8. Mammalia
9. Rodentia
10. Kingdom Animalia, phylum Chordata, subphylum Vertebrata

Pages 158–159
1. Feudal lords developed these private fortress-residences to protect the people inside from attackers during wartimes.
2. a
3. The moat was a massive ditch surrounding a castle that was often filled with water to enhance the security of a castle. The deep water was much more difficult for invaders to travel through rather than simply over land.
4. c
5. They could be stopped in the outer bailey and fired upon by defenders from above.
6. The keep contained the living quarters of the lord and his family, the rooms of state, and the prison cells.
7. The drawbridge could be raised or lowered, and when raised, attackers were unable to enter the castle.
8. Because the castle was planned

for security, the living quarters were rude, poorly lighted, and without provisions for comfort.
9. Answers will vary.
10. Answers will vary.

Pages 160–161
1. the king
2. peasants or serfs
3. probably the king, who had to give up very little compared to the serfs
4. 5th century to the 15th century
5. It would have been good to be a serf because it provided some protection, but serfdom was unpleasant and serfs had very few rights.
6. The serf came under the new lord's rule.
7. land and legal protection
8. land grant
9. security for everyone, including the king
10. stealing

Pages 162–163
1. opinion
2. fact
3. fact
4. opinion
5. fact
6. base, fundament, necessity, requirement
7. It is something that affects a large number of individuals within a population at the same time; possible examples: influenza, smallpox, typhoid fever, tuberculosis, HIV, meningitis, cholera, diptheria.
8. leech
9. Answers will vary, but could include scared, worried, and then lightheaded; disgusted, grossed out
10. bodily fluids
11. It was believed that the humors had to be in balance for a person to remain healthy.

Pages 164–165
1. 5, 4, 2, 3, 1
2. probably in China
3. possible answers: because the flesh of victims would often turn black; because it was such a dark time in history
4. No, it killed people of all social classes.
5. The mosquito can spread malaria.
6. Their populations dropped dramatically.
7. Because of the shortage of labor, workers could charge many times their usual rate for work and would sometimes move to a new lord or noble who offered better incentives and working conditions.
8. The Black Death caused the landowning aristocracy to

lose much of their power and status.

9. antibiotics
10. The country would have been preferable, because some rural areas were spared. Cities suffered the brunt because of a higher rodent population and closer quarters.

Pages 166–167
1. 1347
2. north
3. North Sea
4. 1349
5. before
6. areas spared, at least in part
7. They were likely rural areas.
8. possible answers: Paris, Marseilles, Bordeaux, Avignon, Montpellier, Angers
9. possible answers: Carpathian, Alps, Pyrenees, Taurus
10. Answers will vary.

Page 168–169
1. 1, 3, 2
2. A squire was responsible for dressing the knight for battles and tournaments and taking care of the knight's armor and weapons.
3. He would follow his master on the battlefield to protect him if the knight fell.
4. Answers will vary, but could include scared, nervous, brave, proud, dutiful
5. possible answers: about horses, armor, and weapons; practiced fighting with a sword; use a bow and arrow; manners and social graces; how to sing, play instruments and dance; religious training; read and write
6. part of the induction of a knight in which the new knight was tapped on the shoulders or neck with the flat of the sword
7. The red clothes symbolized his blood, white clothes symbolized purity, and brown clothes symbolized his return to the earth after death.
8. He would have to confess to his sins, take a symbolic bath, and fast to cleanse his soul. He would also have to dress in white and pray all night watching over his weapons and armor.
9. This is the code of conduct a knight promised to uphold. It entailed being brave, loyal, courteous, and protecting the defenseless.
10. He would be stripped of his knighthood and "buried."

Pages 170–171
1. It refers to the shining metal of a knight's armor.

2. chain mail
3. Yes. Thousands of rings were woven together to form one article of chain mail armor.
4. greave
5. couter
6. They allowed him to breathe.
7. 72–92 pounds
8. Yes, he had to carry around all that weight, fight in it, ride a horse in it, and be able to wield a weapon.
9. pauldron
10. gunpowder

Pages 172–173
Answers will vary, but should reflect the indicated part of speech.

Page 174
Stories will vary.

Page 175
Accounts will vary.

Pages 176–177
1. genes
2. Genes do things like tell your body what color to make your eyes and hair.
3. c
4. b
5. dominant allele
6. The earlobe is unattached.
7. The earlobe is unattached.
8. The earlobe is attached.
9. The person can roll his or her tongue.
10. The person can roll his or her tongue
11. The person cannot roll his or her tongue

Pages 178–179
1. He studied of the inheritance of traits in pea plants and discovered laws governing the passage of traits from one living thing to another.
2. father of genetics
3. Mendel's first law states that the a cells of a plant may contain just one of two different traits possible.
4. His second law states that characteristics are inherited independently from another.
5. Mendel's third law states that each inherited characteristic is determined by two hereditary factors, or genes, which decide whether a trait appears or not.
6. Mendel traced the seven basic characteristics of pea plants.
7. They apply to plants as well as people.
8. His work led to the discovery of dominant and recessive traits, the concept of heterozygous and homozygous, and other advanced phenomena.
9. It has identical alleles for a single trait.

10. It has two different alleles for a single trait.

Pages 180–181
1. A genetic disorder is a condition that has some origin in an individual's genetic makeup.
2. true
3. true
4. false
5. false
6. false
7. true
8. false
9. true
10. possible answer: Down's syndrome

Pages 182–183
1. hydrogen (H)
2. 1
3. c
4. gold (Au)
5. a
6. 16
7. groups
8. periods
9. Dmitri I. Mendeleev
10. to extract information about individual elements

Pages 184–185
1.– 4.

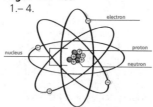

5. negative
6. positive
7. They attract one other.
8. They would repel one another, and the atom would not stick together.
9. the nucleus
10. The number of protons in an atom determines its properties as an element.
11. atomic number